P9-CQI-766

HOW TO THINK
LIKE AN ECONOMIST

Roger A. Arnold

California State University
San Marcos

THOMSON

SOUTH-WESTERN

Australia · Canada · Mexico · Singapore · Spain · United Kingdom · United States

How to Think Like an Economist
Roger A. Arnold

VP/Editorial Director:
Jack W. Calhoun

VP/Editor-in-Chief:
Michael P. Roche

Publisher:
Michael B. Mercier

Acquisitions Editor:
Michael W. Worls

Developmental Editor:
Jennifer E. Baker

Executive Marketing Manager:
Lisa L. Lysne

Production Editor:
Starratt E. Alexander

Manufacturing Coordinator:
Rhonda Utley

Media Developmental Editor:
Peggy Buskey

Media Production Editor:
Pam Wallace

Design Project Manager:
Justin Klefeker

Production House:
Sheridan Publications Services

Cover and Internal Designer:
Justin Klefeker

Cover Images:
© PhotoDisc, © Digital Vision, and © Digital Stock

Printer:
Edwards Bros.—Ann Arbor, MI

COPYRIGHT © 2005
by South-Western, part of the Thomson Corporation. South-Western, Thomson, and the Thomson logo are trademarks used herein under license.

Printed in the United States of America
1 2 3 4 5 07 06 05 04 03

ISBN: 0-324-01575-5

Library of Congress Control Number: 2003115843

ALL RIGHTS RESERVED.

No part of this work covered by the copyright hereon may be reproduced or used in any form or by any means—graphic, electronic, or mechanical, including photocopying, recording, taping, Web distribution or information storage and retrieval systems—without the written permission of the publisher.

For permission to use material from this text or product, submit a request online at http://www.thomsonrights.com.

For more information, contact South-Western, 5191 Natorp Boulevard, Mason, Ohio, 45040. Or you can visit our Internet site at: http://www.swlearning.com

THOMSON

SOUTH-WESTERN

How to Think Like an Economist
Roger A. Arnold

VP/Editorial Director:
Jack W. Calhoun

VP/Editor-in-Chief:
Michael P. Roche

Publisher:
Michael B. Mercier

Acquisitions Editor:
Michael W. Worls

Developmental Editor:
Jennifer E. Baker

Executive Marketing Manager:
Lisa L. Lysne

Production Editor:
Starratt E. Alexander

Manufacturing Coordinator:
Rhonda Utley

Media Developmental Editor:
Peggy Buskey

Media Production Editor:
Pam Wallace

Design Project Manager:
Justin Klefeker

Production House:
Sheridan Publications Services

Cover and Internal Designer:
Justin Klefeker

Cover Images:
© PhotoDisc, © Digital Vision, and © Digital Stock

Printer:
Edwards Bros.—Ann Arbor, MI

COPYRIGHT © 2005
by South-Western, part of the Thomson Corporation. South-Western, Thomson, and the Thomson logo are trademarks used herein under license.

Printed in the United States of America
1 2 3 4 5 07 06 05 04 03

ISBN: 0-324-01575-5

Library of Congress Control Number: 2003115843

ALL RIGHTS RESERVED.

No part of this work covered by the copyright hereon may be reproduced or used in any form or by any means—graphic, electronic, or mechanical, including photocopying, recording, taping, Web distribution or information storage and retrieval systems—without the written permission of the publisher.

For permission to use material from this text or product, submit a request online at http://www.thomsonrights.com.

For more information, contact South-Western, 5191 Natorp Boulevard, Mason, Ohio, 45040. Or you can visit our Internet site at: http://www.swlearning.com

LINCOLN CHRISTIAN COLLEGE AND SEMINARY

Contents

110972

Preface

When I started teaching the economics principles course years ago, I assigned the students a principles text to read. The students and I discussed the material in the book in class, and the students learned what factors can shift a demand curve, how to compute price elasticity of demand, how to figure out whether a firm should continue to produce or should shut down, and many other economic concepts. I was always very excited when I taught the students these things, but somehow they didn't seem excited to be learning about them. At times, they seemed downright bored.

For a while, I blamed the students. I thought they weren't motivated enough to learn economics. Somehow they just couldn't see how useful economics could be to them.

Then, for some unknown reason, I started telling my students certain "economics stories." The stories were designed to communicate to the students how economists think about the world. The students liked listening to the stories, and they actually began to understand the economic approach. They began to understand what it means to "think like an economist."

After the students learned how economists think, I noticed that they started to use economics to analyze their world. They began to enjoy studying and wanted to learn the technical details of economics. Computing price elasticity of demand was no longer an abstract arithmetic exercise, but a means of answering a question the student had formulated.

My experience with economics stories in the classroom changed the way I teach the principles course. I still assign a principles text for the students to read and for us to discuss in class. But I also tell the students the stories in this book. As I tell them the stories, I point out explicitly how each story demonstrates how economists look at and think about the world.

After teaching this way for a few years, I realized that I was wrong to believe that my students weren't motivated enough to want to learn economics. They are motivated to learn what they believe they can use. When students realize how they can use economics, they want to learn all they can.

Teaching using economics stories has also changed another of my beliefs. I used to believe that the most important factor in getting a student to think like an economist is time. Just as a seed needs time to grow into a flower, a student needs time to learn how to think like an economist. How much time? I used to think two years; but I don't think that anymore. I know that it is possible to teach students how to think like economists in 10 to 15 weeks—about one semester.

However, students can't learn to think like economists in one semester by using a large, encyclopedic introductory economics text. Such a text is useful for teaching the details of economics, but not the economic way of thinking.

To teach students how economists think, we must tell them stories. While we tell the stories, we must point out just what is "running through the economist's head." In this book, I have tried to focus on what goes through the economist's head as he or she looks at the world.

I have learned that when I assign a principles text along with the stories in this book, the vast majority of my students learn to use economics and to think like economists in less than 15 weeks.

I used to feel guilty when my students left my class. I felt guilty because they left the classroom not really understanding how to use economics and not really understanding how economists think. I knew I was not really "getting through" to them all the power of economic analysis.

I no longer feel guilty. Today I feel like I am doing the job in the classroom that I am being paid to do. I am helping my students understand the economic approach; I am helping my students use economics and think like economists.

Because I use the stories in this book to explain how economists think, I have less time in class to discuss the details in a principles text. One minute more on the stories in this book necessarily means one less minute spent on the principles text.

But, as economists, we have been trained to compare "what we give up by teaching the principles text one less minute" to "what we gain by teaching the stories in this book one more minute." For the early minutes, I think what we gain is greater than what we lose. Where is the marginal return from discussing the material in each of the two types of books the same? For me, it is when I spend about 80 percent of the semester on the material in a principles book and 20 percent on the material in this book.

This book can be seamlessly integrated into the principles curriculum in a variety of ways to benefit students. For convenience, the following paragraphs describe six different methods of using this book in the economics principles course.

Method 1. Spend the first 12 weeks of a 15-week semester discussing the material in one of the large, encyclopedic principles texts. Spend the last 3 weeks of the semester having students read this book. Assign a few chapters each week. In class, quickly go over the economic principle discussed in each chapter. Then, ask students to explain the principle "in their words" and apply the principle to something not discussed in the book.

Method 2. This method is the same as Method 1 except that instead of having students read this book at the end of the semester, have them read it at the beginning. In other words, use the first 3 weeks of the semester to discuss the material in this book, and then begin the principles-book part of the course.

Method 3. In some introductory economics courses (especially small ones), students are asked to write an eight-to-ten-page research paper that is due sometime near the end of the semester. Assign your students this book, telling them it consists of economics stories that illustrate how economists think. Ask them to read it, and then to write a paper applying at least three of the concepts or principles in the book to analyze something of interest to them. Simply put, ask them to use the material in this book to come up with their own economic applications.

I have used this method, and the results are quite startling. Initially, the students see the task before them as monumental. They often do not know how to go from knowing about several economic principles to coming up with their own applications. But, in time, the students do come up with their own applications and then often say something like this, "I think I learned more economics from that one assignment than from anything else in the course."

Method 4. Assign one to three chapters of this book to different five-person groups. Ask each group to present the assigned chapters to the class. Each group should outline the principle or concept discussed in the chapters and then present an application based on one of the principles discussed in one of the chapters. Afterwards, the students in the class get to ask members of the group any questions they might have based on the presentation.

Method 5. Have students read each chapter on their own. Then use the questions at the end of each chapter to engage students in a classroom discussion.

Method 6. Assign chapters in your chosen principles text and the relevant corresponding chapters in this book during the same week. For example, if your students are reading about price elasticity of demand in their principles text, then you could assign Chapter 17 (which discusses price elasticity of demand) in this book. Or, suppose your students are reading about economic methodology in their principles text. Then you could assign Chapter 3 (on building and testing economic theories) in this book.

The following list of chapters and associated topics may be helpful in planning your course, especially if you choose to use Method 6.

Chapter 1 helps to illustrate "goods" and "bads," utility and disutility, opportunity cost, unintended effects, and tradeoffs.

Chapter 2 helps to illustrate efficiency or optimality and benefits and costs.

Chapter 3 helps to explain how economists build and test theories.

Chapter 4 helps to illuminate unintended effects and the *ceteris paribus* assumption.

Chapter 5 helps to illustrate predicting and explaining in economics.

Chapter 6 demonstrates fungibility.

Chapter 7 helps to illustrate equilibrium and consumer equilibrium.

Chapter 8 explains why the cost of saying you're going to do something is less than the cost of actually doing what you say. This chapter also illustrates the law of demand.

Chapter 9 helps to illustrate the Coase Theorem.

Chapter 10 helps to illustrate relative prices.

Chapter 11 discusses spontaneous orders.

Chapter 12 helps to demonstrate games and game theory.

Chapter 13 illustrates buyers' and sellers' markets.

Chapter 14 demonstrates rationality.

Chapter 15 helps to illustrate scarcity and rationing devices.

Chapter 16 further demonstrates different rationing devices as well as the concepts of scarcity and opportunity cost.

Chapter 17 helps to illustrate price elasticity of demand and total revenue.

Chapter 18 helps to explain how economists ask questions to develop and explore theories and illustrates distortions of the free market. This chapter also touches on market controls, such as price ceilings.

Chapter 19 helps to illustrate trading, transfers, gifts, and rent-seeking.

Chapter 20 helps to illuminate entrepreneurship.

Chapter 21 explains how economists use ratios to obtain a more complete picture of a given setting and illustrates how to determine purchasing power, how firms decide how much of a good to produce and when to shut down and when not to, and much more.

Chapter 22 demonstrates the law of comparative advantage and the law of diminishing marginal utility.

Chapter 23 helps to demonstrate individuals' short-term vs. long-term desires and the constraints we may try to use on ourselves to balance short-term and long-term interests.

Chapter 24 helps to describe self-interested behavior and why what is best for each individual is not necessarily best for a larger group of individuals.

Of course, there are other ways to use this book. I am not sure what the best method is, or even if there is a best method. I do know that using something to complement the encyclopedic principles text is an effective way of getting the economics taught in the principles course to stick. I hope that you find this book the right complement for your courses.

Roger A. Arnold

ABOUT THE AUTHOR

Roger A. Arnold is professor of economics at California State University San Marcos. His writing achievements include academic articles, textbooks, and newspaper columns. He regularly teaches such courses as Principles of Economics, Economic Approach to Politics and Sociology, Money and Banking, Macroeconomic Theory, and Microeconomic Theory. He is the author of two introductory economics textbooks—Microeconomics and Macroeconomics—both in the sixth edition. He lives in Carlsbad, California (25 miles north of San Diego), with his wife, Sheila, and his two sons, Daniel, 16, and David, 13.

chapter 1

Can You Get Too Much of a Good Thing?

In economics, there are goods and bads. A **good** is something that gives someone utility or satisfaction. Food, clothes, entertainment, books, and cars are goods. A **bad**, on the other hand, is something that gives someone disutility or dissatisfaction. Pollution is a bad, as is the flu, the measles, and being in the company of someone you truly dislike.

You have probably heard the saying, "You can never get too much of a good thing." (A "good thing" in everyday speech is simply a "good" in the language of economics. Drop the word "thing.") Do you think it is true that you can never get too much of a good? If you do, then you disagree with economists. To understand why economists disagree with this saying, let's consider good health, which most people believe is a good. People often say you can never get too much good health. Do their actions reflect what they say?

The person who eats a lot of fatty foods, doesn't exercise, and smokes ten cigarettes a day may say she is healthy. But could her health be better? Undoubtedly, her health would improve if she reduced her consumption of fatty foods, exercised moderately, and quit smoking. Suppose she does just that. But given this new status quo, can she improve her health even further? Why not cut out *all* fatty foods? Instead of exercising only moderately, why not exercise more and become even healthier? Surely, most people can take some action to improve their health, even if only by a tiny amount.

Actually, almost no one tries to achieve a perfect state of good health because this perfect state is not easy to achieve. You have to sacrifice and work to achieve it. Specifically, you have to give up too many other good things (goods) to achieve it. You have to give up the benefits you derive from eating a juicy, tasty (but fatty) hamburger, for example. You might choose a little less good health and a tasty hamburger rather than a little more good health and no hamburger. If so, then your actions have told us that there really can be too much of a good thing—or, at least, too much of *one* good thing. And that is what the economist said.

THE PRICE OF A GOOD

You probably prefer a grade of B in a course to a grade of C, and you probably prefer an A to a B. For all students, high grades are a good. But high grades are not given away. You have to work long and hard to get an A. When you consider the work you have to do to get an A, you might prefer to do less work and get a B.

For example, Bob might be capable of earning an A in his biology class if he applies himself and works hard. But he might choose not to do so. He might view the time and effort he has to expend to get the A "too high a price" to pay. Does it follow that if Bob does not spend the time and effort to get an A that he is behaving unreasonably? Not at all. The reason he might not want to spend the time and effort to get an A is that although A's are goods, the world is full of other goods too. And spending time and effort to get one good (such as an A in biology) means one has less time and effort available to get another good (such as socializing with friends).

LIFE IS FULL OF TRADEOFFS

If there were only one good in the world—only one good from which utility or satisfaction could be derived—then there could never be enough of this one good. You would naturally want more and more of it. But, of course, there isn't only *one* good in the world. There are *many* goods. And getting more of one good often means you have to get less of some other good. Getting more good health means getting less of something else that is a good—juicy hamburgers. Getting more A's in your courses means getting less of something else that is a good—socializing with your friends.

The economist captures the essence of this concept by noting that "life is full of tradeoffs." This simply means that more of one good often means less of some other good.

CAN THERE EVER BE TOO LITTLE OF A BAD THING?

Think of the opposite of a good—a bad. As stated earlier, a bad is something that gives people disutility or dissatisfaction. What is the right amount of a bad? Is zero the right amount of a bad?

For example, pollution is something that most people consider a bad. Would it follow that less pollution is preferable to more pollution? In other words, is 100 particles of pollution better than 1,000, and is 10 better than 100, and is zero pollution (no pollution) better than 10 particles of pollution? Certainly that would seem to make sense. But the economist is here to tell us that bads are sometimes connected to goods. The economist might point out that most people consider driving their cars to get from one location to another location to be a good. But driving a car is not a pollution-free activity. Pollution is emitted into the air when a car is driven. We can try to reduce the amount of pollution, but some will still exist. Do you think most people would be willing to give up driving cars in order to have zero pollution? Most people would say that some pollution and driving our cars is a better option than no pollution and not driving our cars. In short, some pollution might be better than no pollution.

ACTIONS SPEAK LOUDER THAN WORDS

Regardless of what people say, their actions express their true views. You might say you believe that you can never get too much of a good thing, that it is better to have no pollution than some pollution, and that high grades are of the utmost importance to you. But these are only words. People's behavior almost never validates the general content of these thoughts.

For example, people might say that there can never be too much of a good thing, but they always act as if there can be. The person who says that you can never be healthy enough eats junk food once in awhile and doesn't always get as much rest as is necessary for good health. The person who says that you can never be safe enough in your house is the same person who installs a bolt on his front door but doesn't buy an alarm system. The person who says that you can never have enough money is the same person who decides not to work overtime or to take on a second job to earn more income.

Through our everyday actions, we clearly state that we know there are tradeoffs in life and there can be too much of a good thing. It's only in our everyday speech that we sometimes forget what we show by our actions that we know to be true.

What the Economist Thinks

- *There is such a thing as too much of a good thing.* The reason the economist thinks this is because he knows that there is more than just one good in life and that getting more of one good often comes at the cost of getting less of another good.

- *There are tradeoffs in life.* As long as there is more than just one good in life, there will be tradeoffs between goods.

Questions to Answer

1. "People will pay to obtain goods and to remove bads." Do you agree or disagree with this statement? Give an example of a person paying to get a good. Give an example of a person paying to remove a bad.

2. "If there were only one good in the world, you could never get enough of this one good." Do you agree or disagree with this statement? Explain your answer.

3. We argued that a student might not want to give up the time and energy required to get an A in a course. He might prefer a B and more time to socialize than an A and less time to socialize. The nature of this argument is that the student chooses which option is better for him. What other reason(s) might explain why a student earns a lower grade than a higher grade?

4. Why do you think a person who says there can never be too much of a good thing often acts differently? In other words, why do people show a difference between their words and their actions?

5. "One thing that makes life so frustrating is that we can't always get more of all the good things in life. I want to eat what I want to eat and have good health, too, but I don't seem to be able to have both. I want more leisure and more income, but again I don't seem to be able to have both. There are just too many tradeoffs (among good things) in life and that frustrates me. I imagine heaven to be a place where there are no such tradeoffs. You can have more of everything that gives you happiness. In heaven, it is possible to eat chocolate cake all day and still lose weight." Comment.

chapter 2

There Is a Right Amount of Everything

The last chapter explains how there can be *too much* of a good thing. No doubt many of us also believe there can be *too little* of a good thing. If there can be too much of a good thing and too little of a good thing, then the right amount of a good thing must be that amount at which there is neither too much nor too little. This concept is reminiscent of *Goldilocks and the Three Bears*: One bed is too hard, one bed is too soft, but one bed is *just right*.

How can we find the right amount of a good thing? In economics, the right amount of a good thing is called the **efficient** or **optimum amount**. Can we use economics to determine the optimum amount of a good thing?

For example, if doughnuts are good things, can we use economics to decide that three doughnuts are too few, eight are too many, and four is the right amount? Unfortunately, economics cannot give this precise an answer. Without specific data, economics cannot be used to determine the optimum number of doughnuts for each person. However, economics does provide a condition by which to measure the right amount of things. But first, we need to distinguish between benefits and costs and between total and marginal magnitudes.

BENEFITS AND COSTS

Many activities come with both benefits and costs. The benefits are those things that make us better off or that raise our level of satisfaction. For example, the benefits of exercise might be a healthier body and more energy.

The costs of an activity are always viewed by economists as "opportunities foregone"—what one gives up to perform the activity—and are referred to by economists as **opportunity costs**. For example, the opportunity cost of exercising is what you would be doing if you weren't exercising. If what you would be doing is reading a book, then reading a book is the cost of exercising. If what you would be doing is working at a job earning $40 an hour, then working at a job earning $40 an hour is the cost of exercising.

TOTAL AND MARGINAL MAGNITUDES

Total refers to "all" and marginal refers to "additional." Economists look at the total and marginal benefits of an activity.

For example, suppose you are studying for a biology test. The total benefits of studying for the test equal the sum of the benefits derived from studying each minute of five hours. In other words, total benefits are "all" the benefits associated with studying. The marginal benefits of studying for the test are the "additional" benefits of studying an additional unit of time—say, an additional minute.

Think of total benefits and marginal benefits in dollar terms. For example, the total benefits of studying for all five hours might equal $100, but the marginal benefits of studying for one minute more—say, studying from the tenth minute to the eleventh minute—might equal 20 cents.

Economists also view costs in total and marginal terms. In other words, the total costs of an activity are "all" the costs associated with the activity and the marginal costs of an activity are the "additional" costs associated with an additional amount of the activity. The total costs of studying for five hours might be $100, but the marginal costs of studying for one minute more—again, say, studying from the tenth minute to the eleventh minute—might equal 14 cents.

FINDING THE OPTIMUM BY THINKING IN TERMS OF MARGINAL BENEFITS AND MARGINAL COSTS

What is the right—or optimum—amount of a good? If watching television is a good, what is the optimum amount of time to watch television? If eating doughnuts is a good, what is the optimum number of doughnuts to eat? If playing baseball is a good, what is the optimum amount of time to play baseball?

The optimum amount of anything is that amount at which the marginal benefits equal the marginal costs. Anything less is too little and anything more is too much.

To illustrate, suppose you have been watching a baseball game on television for 76 minutes. Is it worth watching the game for one more minute? Well, the answer is yes if for you, the marginal benefits (additional benefits) of watching the game are greater than the marginal costs (additional costs). In other words, you are likely to keep watching the game as long as for every additional minute you perceive marginal benefits greater than marginal costs. You will stop watching the game when the two are equal. And you will never watch the game if you expect the marginal costs to be greater than the marginal benefits.

HITTING YOURSELF IN THE HEAD WITH A HAMMER

Although many activities come with both benefits and costs, some do not. For example, it is hard to see what benefits you would receive from hitting yourself in the head with a hammer (unless, of course, you want someone to question your mental stability). However, there are clearly costs to hitting yourself in the head. So, there are no benefits and some costs.

What is the optimum amount of hitting yourself in the head with a hammer? Is it three blows to the head, one blow, or none? Obviously, the right answer is none. Recall that one only continues an activity when the marginal benefits are greater than the marginal costs. In this example, though, there are no benefits and only costs, so marginal benefits would never be greater than marginal costs. The optimum amount of hitting yourself in the head with a hammer is zero.

THE RIGHT AMOUNT OF TIME TO PLAY TENNIS

Some activities, such as watching a baseball game or hitting yourself in the head with a hammer, only require one person. However, other activities require more than one person. One activity that requires more than one person is tennis.

Let's consider John and Susie, who get together to play tennis. For John, there are both benefits and costs to playing tennis. The benefits might be fun and exercise. The costs are the benefits that John forfeits by not doing what he would be doing if he weren't playing tennis. For example, if he would be receiving the benefits of reading a good book if he weren't playing tennis, then these benefits (which he forfeits at this time) are the costs of playing tennis. Similarly, for Susie, there are both benefits and costs to playing tennis.

Is the right amount of tennis for John the same as the right amount for Susie? For example, we know that John will want to continue playing tennis as long as the marginal benefits of tennis are greater than the marginal costs. He will stop when the marginal benefits are equal to the marginal costs. Let's say this time amounts to 60 minutes after he first starts playing tennis.

Susie, like John, will want to continue playing tennis as long as the marginal benefits she derives from playing tennis are greater than her marginal costs of playing tennis. She will stop when the marginal benefits are equal to the marginal costs. Let's say this time amounts to 40 minutes after she first starts playing tennis.

So, in other words, the right amount of tennis for John is longer (20 minutes longer) than the right amount of tennis for Susie. Before we continue, ask yourself why Susie wants to play less tennis than John. A very general answer is that the benefits and costs of tennis are not the same for Susie as they are for John. If the benefits and costs were the same for both, the right amount of time to play tennis would be the same for both. But Susie wants to play less tennis, so either her benefits of tennis are not as high as John's benefits of tennis or her costs of tennis are not as low as John's. In short, compared to John, Susie incurs either lower benefits or higher costs of playing tennis.

Now suppose 40 minutes have passed since Susie and John started playing tennis, and Susie says she wants to quit playing. But John wants to play more tennis. If he stops playing now, he will stop 20 minutes too early as far as he is concerned. Instead of getting in the right amount of tennis, he will end up with too little tennis.

What might John do to move toward his right amount of tennis (which is more tennis than Susie currently wants to play)? John might try to either raise Susie's benefits of playing more tennis or lower her costs. Their conversation might be something like the following:

> **Susie:** We'd better stop playing. I really should be going.
>
> **John:** Where do you have to go?
>
> **Susie:** I need to go to the library and start working on a paper I have to write for my Spanish lit class. [Susie is telling us something about the costs to her of continuing to play tennis; namely, she will fall behind in her course work.]
>
> **John:** Do you have to do that right now? [John wouldn't say this if he had already played his right amount of tennis.]
>
> **Susie:** I'd better. If I don't, I'm going to fall behind. I hate to get into that fix.
>
> **John:** Let's play a little longer. Later both of us can go to the library, and I'll help you do the research for your paper. [John is trying to lower the cost to Susie of staying and playing tennis a little while longer.]

John might or might not be successful at lowering the cost to Susie of continuing to play tennis (at least for 20 more minutes). But, John's success or failure is not relevant. The point is that if he hasn't yet achieved his right amount of tennis playing, he must either try to raise the benefits to Susie of continuing to play tennis, or to lower her costs, or to do some of each.

A VIEW OF LIFE

Think of all the things you do in a day, week, or month. You study, attend classes, drive a car, talk with your friends, buy clothes, work, listen to music, watch television, brush your teeth, and so on. You do literally hundreds of different things. According to economists, there is an optimum amount of time to spend doing each of these activities. There is an optimum amount of time to study, to sleep, to brush your teeth, to talk with a friend on the phone.

Now ask yourself if you spend the right (optimum) amount of time on all the activities you do. For example, let's say that you did activities *A–Z* during the last 30 days. Did you do the right amount of each of these activities? Or do you think you might have done the right amount of activities *A–R*, too much of activities *S–V*, and too little of activities *W–Z*? Our guess is that you believe you did not do the right amount of each activity. Instead, you believe you did the right amount of some activities, too much of some, and too little of others. If this is the case—you haven't done the right amount of all activities—what will you do? The economist's answer is that you will try to do more of those activities on which you have spent too little time and you will try to do less of those activities on which you have spent too much time.

In short, your life consists of daily trying to spend the optimum amount of time on all your activities. You will try to repeat exactly those activities on which you feel you are spending the right amount of time, do more of those activities on which you feel you have spent too little time, and do less of those activities on which you feel you have spent too much time. Consider an example to illustrate this point. Most people do not spend either more or less time brushing their teeth than they did the day before. They have already determined their right amount of time for brushing their teeth, and this amount doesn't seem to change from day to day (although it may increase a little a week before a person has to visit the dentist).

But for exercising, watching television, or spending money on clothes, people seem to be adjusting their time. One person may believe she spends too little time exercising and try to increase the time. Another person may believe he spends too much time watching television and try to cut back. In all cases, economists believe that people are trying to adjust to the right amount.

One other wrinkle needs to be ironed out. Is it possible that the right amount for one activity in one week will change in the next week? For example, might two hours of reading one week be the right amount of reading for that week but be too little for the next week? The answer is yes. But before this can be the case, something has to change between the weeks; specifically, the costs or the benefits of reading have to change. Many things can change the benefits and costs of reading, sleeping, eating, studying, or anything else for that matter. But one of the main things that can change benefits and costs is new information.

To illustrate, consider the costs and benefits of smoking cigarettes. Many years ago, people didn't know that the costs of smoking cigarettes were as high as they have turned out to be. They didn't know, for example, that smoking cigarettes increased one's probability of getting lung cancer. When that information came out, many people immediately saw the costs of smoking rise and compared the new higher costs of smoking to the benefits they derived from smoking. For many people, the costs rose high enough that they surpassed the benefits of smoking, and so they stopped smoking.

What the Economist Thinks

- *There is a right amount of everything.* Specifically, the right amount is neither too much nor too little. It is the amount at which the marginal benefits of something equal the marginal costs of that something. For an economist, the right amount is the efficient or optimum amount.

- *Life consists of daily trying to do the optimum amount of all activities.* People try to repeat exactly those activities on which they feel they are spending the right amount of time, do more of those activities on which they feel they have spent too little time, and do less of those activities on which they feel they have spent too much time.

- *The right amount of something may change from time to time.* This occurs if either the costs or the benefits of that something change.

- *New information can change the way people perceive the benefits and costs of various activities.*

Questions to Answer

1. This chapter discusses activities that you can do by yourself (watching a baseball game on television) and activities that you can do only with someone else (playing tennis). Would you expect to be more frustrated in those activities you can do by yourself or in those activities you can do only with another person? Explain your answer and then give three examples of both types of activities.

2. Two people get married, and then seven years later, they get divorced. What happened?

3. A person will try to reduce the amount of something if he believes he has too much of it. If he can't reduce it himself, do you think he will seek help from someone else to get rid of it? Why or why not? Give an example of a person seeking help from someone else to get rid of something he has too much of and can't get less of himself.

4. Suzanne read for two hours a day when she had relatively poor eyesight. Then, when she got prescription eyeglasses that corrected her vision to 20/20, she began to read three hours a day. For her, the right amount of reading changed when the costs of reading decreased, which was the case when she received her prescription eyeglasses. Give an example of an activity where the right amount of it changed when either the benefits or the costs of that activity changed.

5. What will make the "average person" nicer than he or she already is?

chapter 3

Have a Question, Build a Theory

What do you do when you have a question about something that interests you? Do you ask a friend or a professor? Do you check on the Internet to see if you can find some information about the topic? What do you think an economist would do in this situation? When an economist has a question about something that interests her, she tries to find the answer to her question by building a theory, making predictions, and then testing the theory.

Let's consider Jones, an economist who is interested in why the crime rate (for certain types of crime) is higher in the United States than in England. Jones will begin to build his theory by trying to identify the key variables that he believes influence the crime rate. **Key variables** are those variables that an economist believes explain *most* of what he or she is trying to explain (in this case, the crime rate). By focusing on the key variables, and only on the key variables, the economist necessarily leaves out certain variables. To illustrate, suppose Jones thinks there are 15 variables, *A–O*, that may have something to do with the crime rate. However, of the 15 variables, he thinks that some variables are important and some are not so important. Assume in this case that Jones thinks variables *B*, *G*, and *H* are very important and the other variables are not so important. This means Jones thinks that variables *B*, *G*, and *H* together explain *most* of what he is trying to explain about the difference in the crime rate. For example, he might think these three variables explain 99 percent of what he is trying to explain. That's close enough to 100 percent for Jones not to be too concerned about the other variables.

After Jones has identified his key variables, he will hypothesize about how they affect the crime rate. For example, he may say that if variable *B* increases, the crime rate is predicted to increase. Or if variable *G* decreases, the crime rate is predicted to decrease.

Next, Jones will try to test his theory by finding out whether or not it predicts correctly. Testing a theory is an important step for an economist. A layperson will often assume something is correct if it "sounds right." An economist knows that people often accept something as true—when it is not—simply because it sounds correct.

To illustrate, imagine that you are a contemporary of Christopher Columbus. At that time, many people said that the earth was flat. If you had lived then, what would you have said? It is likely that you, too, would have said that the earth was flat. After all, everyday experiences and our senses seem to suggest that it is. But of course, we know today that the earth is not flat. Our point is that what might have sounded correct had we lived at the time of Christopher Columbus turned out to be very wrong.

As another example, imagine you live in a time when people do not know that microorganisms cause sickness. If someone told you that the reason you have the flu is because of these tiny little germs you cannot see, you might have thought the person was crazy. Certainly at one time, talking about invisible germs would seem as crazy as talking today about an invisible rabbit that dances. Thus, we can understand today as correct an explanation that would have sounded completely ridiculous at one time.

These examples suggest that in order to establish truth we need something other than how things sound or appear to us. We need evidence.

IF YOU ARE RIGHT, THEN YOU SHOULD SEE ...

How do we know that what we are thinking is true? Essentially, we know when there is evidence confirming what we believe to be true. For example, suppose Smith builds a theory that predicts all swans are white. If Smith and others then go out into the world and find as many swans as they can and all those swans are white, then Smith can claim that so far the evidence fails to reject her theory. We have deliberately used the cumbersome phrase "the evidence fails to reject her theory," instead of saying "the evidence proves her theory," because some yellow or green or purple swan that Smith did not see might exist in the world. She might have seen only the white swans, and some other color swans might exist that she didn't see.

Of course, only one piece of contrary evidence will reject a theory. For example, if Smith had found only one nonwhite swan, her theory would have been rejected. After all, her theory said that all swans are white.

We can summarize this discussion in simpler terms. When testing a theory, we simply state, "If our theory is right, then we should see _____." Then we fill in the blank with what we should see. In the swan example, we fill in the words "only white swans." And, then, we address the other side of the coin by adding, "If our theory is wrong, then we should see _____." In the swan example, we fill in the words "at least one swan that is not white."

THERE IS CAUSE FOR CONCERN IF A THEORY CANNOT BE FALSIFIED

Notice that there were two parts to testing the swan theory. The first part addressed what we should see if the theory is correct, and the second part addressed what we should see if the theory is not correct. If the theory is correct, we should see all white swans. If the theory is incorrect, we should see at least one nonwhite swan.

Now, let's compare the white swan theory with another theory. Consider a theory that says that everything that happens in the world—a leaf falling, the election of the President of the United States, the C+ a student receives on a mathematics test, a person dying in a car wreck—happens because some computer engineer has written a software program to make it happen. We'll call this theory the Matrix-makes-everything-happen theory (after the movie, *The Matrix*).

Now ask yourself what we would expect to see if the theory is correct. A person may simply answer that everything we see confirms the theory. But this isn't really a very good answer. The reason this is not a very good answer is not immediately obvious, though. We suggest the reason it is not a good answer can be ascertained indirectly.

Consider the fill-in-the-blank exercise again. Ask a proponent of the Matrix-makes-everything-happen theory to complete this statement: "If the Matrix-makes-everything-happen theory is correct, we should see _____." Then, ask an opponent of the theory to complete this statement: "If the Matrix-makes-everything-happen theory is incorrect, we should see _____."

Although both the proponent and the opponent of the theory might not complete their respective sentences the same way, it is highly likely that they will. And that's the point. If two people, taking different sides of an issue, can fill in their respective statements the same way and neither seems to be incorrect, then something is wrong. After all, isn't it odd that the same "evidence" can "fail to reject" and "reject" a theory at the same time?

This situation was impossible in the white swan theory. You can't complete the sentence, "If the white swan theory is correct, we should see _____," the same way you complete the sentence, "If the white swan theory is incorrect, we should see _____." The first statement can clearly only be completed one way: with the words "only white swans." And the second statement can clearly only be completed one way, the direct opposite of what completed the first statement: with the words "at least one nonwhite swan."

Thus, in the white swan theory, the evidence used to "fail to reject" the theory is not the same as the evidence used to "reject" the theory. That is how it should be if things are to make sense. That is how it should be if a theory is capable of being established as true or as not true.

What the Economist Thinks

- *The best way to approach questions (that are not easily answered) is to build and test relevant theories.* For example, by building and testing a theory to answer the question, "Why is the crime rate higher in the United States than in England?" an economist produces rigorous, analytical, and, in the end, more productive results.

- *Some key variables need to be identified when explaining anything.*

- *Accepting a theory because it sounds right is a bad idea.*

- *Testing a theory to see if the evidence rejects or fails to reject it is a good idea.*

- *If the same "evidence" can both reject and fail to reject a theory, we cannot establish the truth or falsity of the theory.*

Questions to Answer

1. Theory *X* does not consider all the variables that might explain what it seeks to explain. Someone criticizes the theory and the theorist (who built the theory) for leaving out certain things. Is this a good criticism of theory *X*? Why or why not?

2. Give an example of an explanation for something that at one time sounded correct to you but that later you learned was not correct. What does this teach you?

3. Many people have theories to explain everyday things even though they don't realize they have these theories. For example, a person might have a theory that seeks to explain why his girlfriend just broke up with him, or why his boss likes him, or why he failed a test. People don't build theories only to explain major phenomena, such as why the universe exists, why gravity works, or why the earth sometimes quakes in California. People build theories to explain things that are not obvious to them but which interest them. What have you tried to explain by building a theory? How do you try to determine whether your theories are correct or not?

4. "The data we have obtained supports theory *X*." "The data we have obtained proves theory *X*." Which of the two statements would a scientist be more likely to use and why?

5. "A theory that explains everything, explains nothing." Do you agree or disagree with this statement? Explain your answer.

chapter 4

Change Often Begets Change

Mandatory seatbelt laws are enacted to try to reduce the number of people killed or seriously injured in car accidents. These laws are based on the fact that people involved in a car accident are less likely to die or to be seriously hurt when they are wearing seatbelts than when they are not wearing seatbelts. If you believe, as many people do, that mandatory seatbelt laws will reduce the number of people killed or seriously injured in accidents, then you have made an implicit assumption. You are assuming that a driver drives the same way when wearing a seatbelt as when not wearing a seatbelt. An economist would not automatically make this assumption because an economist believes that one change often begets another change.

THE WAY THINGS COULD BE

Suppose that on Tuesday, Karen does not bother to fasten her seatbelt when she sets out in her car. Without her seatbelt fastened, she feels less safe and decides to drive very carefully. She obeys every speed limit, she makes a full stop at every stop sign, and she gives plenty of notice to the cars behind her before she changes lanes.

Then on Wednesday, Karen fastens her seatbelt when she gets in her car. As soon as the belt clicks into place, she feels safer than she does when she doesn't wear her seatbelt. This extra sense of safety causes Karen to take a few extra risks. She drives a little faster, she doesn't come to a full stop at every stop sign, and she occasionally changes lanes without giving much notice to the cars behind her.

We are postulating here that Karen's driving behavior is a function of how safe she feels in her car. If she feels relatively unsafe, she drives more carefully than when she feels very safe. Might a person actually behave this way?

Before you answer, consider your own behavior. Suppose when you drove a car you could be 100 percent sure you would not be hurt if you had an accident. Compare how you might drive in this situation with how you would drive if you thought there was at least a 50–50 chance of your being severely hurt if you had an accident. Our guess is that you would drive more carefully—more safely—when you thought there was some positive probability of being hurt than when you thought there was no chance of being hurt.

If you agree and believe your driving behavior might be different in the two different settings, then might it also be different for Karen? Might Karen drive more carefully when she feels less safe (does not wear her seatbelt) than when she feels safe (wears her seatbelt)? If the answer is yes, then we have to look in a different way at the belief that mandatory seatbelt laws will save lives.

Clearly, if people do not change their driving behavior, then wearing seatbelts will necessarily save lives. But if people drive less carefully wearing seatbelts than not wearing seatbelts, then it is not clear that mandatory seatbelt laws will save lives.

We can analyze the situation using an equation. The total number of driver deaths from car accidents equals the number of accidents times the average number of drivers who die per accident.

Total number of driver deaths from car accidents =
Number of accidents × Average number of drivers
who die per accident

Suppose without seatbelts there are 1,000 accidents and an average of 0.20 driver deaths per accident. It follows that there are 200 deaths. Now those persons who believe that seatbelts save lives correctly believe that seatbelts lower the average number of drivers who die per accident. For example, if the average number of drivers who die per accident falls from 0.20 to 0.10 and the number of accidents stays at 1,000 accidents, then the total number of driver deaths falls to 100.

However, lowering the average number of drivers who die per accident only translates into a lower total number of driver deaths *if the number of accidents stays the same.* But the number of accidents might not stay constant. If people really do feel safer wearing seatbelts than not and, consequently, take some risks they ordinarily would not, then the number of accidents might rise. Suppose the number of accidents rises from 1,000 to 2,000 as the average number of drivers who die per accident falls from 0.20 to 0.10. Then, the total number of driver deaths stays constant at 200. In other words, seatbelts lower the average number of drivers who die per accident, but they do not lower the total number of driver deaths from car accidents.

This conclusion is counterintuitive, and the layperson does not readily reach it. But the economist does because the economist is trained to think, "one change often begets another change." In other words, the economist realizes that changing from not wearing a seatbelt to wearing a seatbelt might cause drivers to feel safer and that feeling safer might cause drivers to take some risks they ordinarily wouldn't take when they felt less safe. Thus, the economist realizes that mandatory seatbelt laws might not result in fewer drivers being killed or seriously injured in car accidents.

WHY DIETERS OFTEN DON'T LOSE WEIGHT

William has gained a few pounds lately and is worried about his weight. His trousers are too tight and he generally doesn't like the way he looks. He blames his weight gain on all the ice cream he has been eating recently. So, William decides to change from eating regular (high-fat, high-calorie) ice cream to eating low-fat (low-calorie) ice cream. Will William lose weight as a result of his change from eating one type of ice cream to eating another kind?

The answer most people will give is yes because they implicitly assume the only thing that changes is the type of ice cream that William eats. But often this assumption is incorrect. Many dieters admit to being deceived by low-calorie ice cream and to eating more of it than they would have eaten of regular (high-calorie) ice cream. For example, if William ordinarily ate one bowl of ice cream a day when he was eating regular ice cream, he might eat two bowls a day when he is eating low-fat, low-calorie ice cream. Again, let's look at the situation in terms of an equation.

$$\text{Total calories consumed} = \text{Number of bowls of ice cream} \times \text{Calories per bowl}$$

The low-fat ice cream lowers the calories per bowl. But the total calories consumed will decline *only if* the number of bowls of ice cream stays constant. Suppose the number of bowls increases. If the percentage increase in the number of bowls is greater than the percentage decrease in the calories per bowl, then the total calories consumed will rise.

PRICE CEILINGS

Ask a person on the street if he'd rather pay a lower price for a good than a higher price, and the answer likely will be yes. Most people implicitly believe that a change in price (from high to low) does not beget any other change. But economists know this might not be the case.

Suppose we change an equilibrium price of, say, $10 to a legislated price of, say, $7. (A legislated price that is below the equilibrium price is called a **price ceiling**.) When this occurs, then something will exist when the price is $7 that does not exist when the price is $10—a shortage. In other words, at $10, quantity demanded equals quantity supplied, but at $7, quantity demanded will be greater than quantity supplied. There will be a shortage.

Now if there is a shortage—and the price cannot legally rise to its equilibrium level (which it can't when there is a price ceiling)—then some nonprice rationing device is guaranteed to enter the picture. The most likely rationing device is **first-come-first-served**, which will produce relatively long lines of people waiting to buy the product at $7. Consequently, the time cost (spent in the long line) has to be added to the dollar price of the good to find the full cost of the good.

Suppose that when the price of the good is $10, the time cost is 5 minutes; so, the full cost of the good (dollar price plus time cost) is $10 plus 5 minutes. At a price of $7 and a shortage, the time cost might be 45 minutes; and even then, the person might not be able to purchase the good (after all, quantity demanded is greater than quantity supplied). The full cost of the good then is $7 plus 45 minutes. It is not clear that everyone prefers a dollar price of $7 plus a 45-minute wait (and the chance of not getting the good) to a dollar price of $10 and a 5-minute wait.

The lesson: Change one thing (the price of a good) and something else might change too (the time cost of obtaining the good).

ONE CHANGE BEGETS ANOTHER CHANGE BEGETS THE NEED FOR EMPIRICAL EVIDENCE

Many people make incorrect predictions because they do not realize that one change often produces another change. Many people adamantly believe that wearing seatbelts has to save lives, that eating low-fat, low-calorie ice cream instead of high-fat, high-calorie ice cream has to result in weight loss, and that a lower price for a good must result in a lower total cost to the consumer.

However, as this chapter points out, one change sometimes prompts another change, the latter change might reverse the original change, and the final result is not necessarily clear. One change moves us up, the other change moves us down, so how do we come out on net: up or down? Well, it depends on how high up we went relative to how far down we went. If we went further up than down, then on net, we end up higher than where we started. If we went further down than up, then on net, we end up lower than where we started. And, of course, if we go as far up as down, we end up where we started. It all depends on the degree of change in one variable relative to the degree of change in another variable.

We can be pretty sure that when we use the words "it all depends" in discussing an economic topic, we need empirical evidence to reach a conclusion. Theory alone is insufficient. In this case, knowing only the directional changes in variables is insufficient. We need to measure *how much* the variables move in each direction.

In our seatbelt example, we need to know by how much the average number of driver deaths per accident falls relative to how many more accidents there are. If the number of accidents rises by, say, 2 percent at the same time that the average number of driver deaths per accident falls by 25 percent, then on net, wearing seatbelts ends up saving lives; wearing seatbelts lowers the total number of driver deaths from car accidents.

The point is that we can't know this result beforehand. We need the empirical evidence to determine the net effect of wearing seatbelts.

To Tell the Whole Story, We Need to Identify All the Changes

The economist knows the importance of telling the whole story rather than telling only half the story. Suppose something changes in the world that affects A, B, C, and D. If we identify only the changes to A and B, we have told only half the story. If we identify the changes to A, B, C, and D, then we have told the whole story.

People often do not see the whole story—they do not see all the effects brought about by a single change. People see that wearing seatbelts lowers the average number of driver deaths per accident, but they don't see that the number of accidents might change too. People see that eating low-fat, low-calorie ice cream lowers the number of calories per bowl of ice cream, but they don't see that the number of bowls eaten might also change.

What is the lesson? We must be diligent in order to identify *all* the ripples in the lake produced by the stone thrown into it. We do this by constantly asking ourselves: So, we have identified one change, but are there others?

A story told by Henry Hazlitt, an economist and journalist, in his book *Economics In One Lesson* emphasizes this lesson. One day a young boy throws a rock through a baker's window. The townspeople gather and bemoan the fact that juvenile delinquency is on the rise. But, then, one of the townspeople says that the broken window may actually be a good thing. The baker will have to buy a new window from the glass maker; therefore, the glass maker will be better off—he will have more income. He will spend some of this extra income by buying a new suit of clothes, so the clothes maker will now have more income. And the clothes maker will then spend some of his extra income on a new piece of furniture, so the furniture maker will now have more income. A rock thrown through a glass window, in other words, generates additional income for many people. Can it really have been that bad of an act?

What is overlooked, as Hazlitt points out, is that while the rock through the window changed the baker's consumption pattern in the direction of buying a window, it necessarily changed the baker's consumption pattern away from something else. Perhaps if the baker hadn't spent the money to buy a new window, he would have spent the money to buy a new television set. So now the income that the television manufacturer would have earned is not earned, and so on. In short, we have more purchases in one area (more windows, clothes, and furniture) but fewer purchases in another (television sets and so on).

The more often we tell these kinds of stories, the more often we can see the importance of identifying all the changes and not only some. Still, we can easily forget and tell our stories the way we initially think they should be told. To guard against this, remember the economist's suggestion: Always ask if there is another change that is waiting to be identified.

What the Economist Thinks

- *Rarely does one thing change without changing something else.*
- *To tell the whole story, identify all the changes.*
- *Empirical evidence is often needed to determine the net effect of a change in some variable.*

Questions to Answer

1. Assume that when every driver wears a seatbelt there are fewer driver deaths from car accidents than when every driver does not wear a seatbelt. Does it follow that wearing seatbelts does not increase the number of car accidents? Explain your answer.

2. When would consumers prefer lower prices to higher prices? When would consumers prefer higher prices to lower prices?

3. Smith says that a cut in income tax rates will raise income tax revenues, and Jones says a cut in income tax rates will lower income tax revenues. Who do you agree with and why? Identify any implicit assumptions you make in reaching your conclusion.

4. In the seatbelt example, we hypothesized that the wearing of seatbelts would change two factors in opposite directions. Specifically, the driver deaths per car accident would decrease and the number of car accidents would increase. What happens to the total number of driver deaths depends then on how much each factor changes relative to the other factor. Describe an example from your life where a change in one factor causes two factors to change in opposite directions and the net effect depends on how much each factor changes relative to the other factor.

5. "If a change in one factor (such as A) is the catalyst for a change in two additional factors (such as B and C) and the two additional factors change in opposite directions, then empirical evidence is needed to determine the net effect of the change in the original factor." Do you agree or disagree with this statement? Explain your answer.

chapter 5

Why Is It Harder to Predict Than to Explain?

Suppose you have completed a few courses in economics and are home for summer break. At a family gathering, a relative who has been talking to you about your courses says, "I've noticed that housing prices have been rising recently. Is this going to continue for the next year to 18 months?"

Your relative is asking you to make a prediction. She wants to know what you predict housing prices will do in the next year to 18 months. Will they continue to go up, turn down, or remain constant?

In your economics classes, predicting price changes in competitive markets is easy after you learn the basics of supply and demand. Supply and demand determine prices in competitive markets. For example, if the demand for a good rises and the supply remains constant, price rises. If the demand for a good falls and the supply remains constant, price falls.

But the reason these predictions are easy in the classroom is that the changes in supply and demand are always specified or given to you. In the real world, we don't have this critical information; we don't know how supply and demand might change. So in the real world, we have to predict what will happen to supply and demand.

WHAT DO YOU NEED TO KNOW TO MAKE A PREDICTION?

Let's look again at the original question about housing prices. Your relative asks you to predict what will happen to housing prices. This is the same as asking you to predict what will happen to the supply of houses and to the demand for houses. We identify 13 possibilities for supply and demand:

1. Demand rises and supply does not change

2. Demand rises and supply rises by more (than demand rises)

3. Demand rises and supply rises by less

4. Demand rises and supply rises by the same amount

5. Demand rises and supply falls

6. Demand falls and supply does not change

7. Demand falls and supply falls by more

8. Demand falls and supply falls by less

9. Demand falls and supply falls by the same amount

10. Demand falls and supply rises

11. Demand does not change and supply rises

12. Demand does not change and supply falls

13. Demand does not change and supply does not change

Which of these 13 possibilities will occur? To answer this question, you have to know all the factors that affect supply and demand. For example, demand is a function of, or depends on, changes in population, changes in the money supply, changes in the prices of substitutes, changes in the prices of complementary goods, changes in the age distribution of the population, changes in expectations of future prices, changes in income, and so on. Supply is a function of, or depends on, changes in technology, changes in productivity, changes in taxes, changes in the number of suppliers in a region, changes in the prices of relevant resources (for houses, relevant resources include wood, concrete, plumbing fixtures, and so on), and much more. In short, to predict changes in supply and demand, and therefore prices, you need access to information about all the factors that supply and demand depend on—changes in the money supply, changes in relevant resource prices, and so on.

But that's not all you need. Let's suppose that somehow you have access to all the data you need. You know if relevant resource prices are rising or falling, if productivity (in the house-building industry) is rising or falling, and so on. You still have an immense problem. You don't know for sure whether one of the variables that affects supply does so by more than or less than one of the variables that affects demand.

To illustrate, suppose that as the money supply rises, the demand for houses rises, and that as productivity rises, the supply of houses rises. Furthermore, suppose the only two things happening in the world are that the money supply is rising and productivity is rising. From this information, you could predict that the demand for houses will rise and that the supply of houses will rise too. But this information is still not enough to predict what will happen to housing prices. In this case, housing prices depend on whether the demand for houses rises by more than, less than, or the same amount as the supply of houses rises. In other words, you need to know whether the money-supply effect on the demand for houses is going to be stronger than, less strong than, or as strong as the productivity effect on the supply of houses.

Let's recap what you need know to make an accurate prediction with respect to housing prices.

1. You need to know that housing prices are a function of the demand for and supply of houses. You can learn this in any economics course.

2. You need to know the various combinations of supply and demand that can arise. We noted these 13 possibilities earlier. Again, you can learn this information in any economics course.

3. You need to know what factors influence supply and what factors influence demand. You can learn this in any economics course.

4. You need current information about all the factors that can influence the supply of and demand for houses. In other words, you need to know what is happening to the money supply, productivity, relevant resource prices, the population, expectations with respect to future prices, and so on. This information is difficult to obtain; and even if you could obtain it, the information is not always likely to be accurate.

5. You need to know the strength of one effect compared to another, especially when effects do not influence housing prices in the same direction. This is our money supply-productivity example. The money supply rises and increases the demand for houses, and productivity rises and increases the supply of houses. By itself, an increase in demand raises prices. By itself, an increase in supply lowers prices. Because neither demand nor supply is operating by itself, opposing forces are acting on housing prices. Which force "wins"? It depends on the strength of the money-supply effect on demand in comparison with the productivity effect on supply. However, information about the strength of various effects is not easy to ascertain. Without this information, though, it will be difficult to accurately predict the effect on housing prices.

Our conclusion is that because of the stiff information requirements necessary to make accurate predictions, accurate predictions are hard to make on a consistent basis. Even with an excellent knowledge of supply and demand analysis, you will have a hard time consistently predicting prices because you will likely have less than full information.

WHAT DO YOU NEED TO KNOW TO GIVE AN EXPLANATION?

Suppose that a year to 18 months have passed and housing prices have gone up. Now, someone asks you, "Why did housing prices go up?" Here the person is asking for an explanation, not a prediction. Correct explanations are easier to make than correct predictions are because you need less information to make a correct explanation.

Look back at our list of 13 possibilities. Not all 13 possibilities are consistent with rising prices, only 5 are: numbers 1, 3, 5, 7, and 12. For example, number 1 is "demand rises and supply does not change," and number 3 is "demand rises and supply rises by less." Both these conditions will result in rising prices.

One way to see how much easier it is to make a correct explanation than a correct prediction is to analyze the situation from the perspective of guessing. If someone asks you to predict the combination of supply and demand forces that will operate in the next year to 18 months in the housing market, you have 1 chance in 13 of guessing correctly. This is a success rate of approximately 7.7 percent. However, if someone asks you to choose the combination of supply and demand forces that must have been operative over the past year to 18 months to explain a rise in housing prices, you have 1 chance in 5 of guessing correctly. This is a 20 percent success rate.

Now let's consider the information you need to give an explanation. Recall the five configurations of changes in supply and demand that can explain rising housing prices: numbers 1, 3, 5, 7, and 12. Three of these configurations (1, 3, and 5) express rising demand, and three (5, 7, and 12) express falling supply. You now need information about the variables that have the effect of either raising demand or lowering supply. If you find information about even one of these variables, then you can automatically eliminate at least two possible explanations of rising prices.

For example, if you learn that the money supply increased, then you know that demand was rising. In this case, you can automatically eliminate possibilities 7 and 12 because number 7 specifies falling demand and number 12 specifies unchanging demand. Or if you learn that productivity was rising, then you know that supply was rising. In this case, you can automatically eliminate possibilities 1, 5, 7, and 12 because in number 1, supply is unchanged and in numbers 5, 7, and 12, supply is falling. In this case, only number 3 can be the correct explanation: If productivity was rising, then supply was rising, and the only way for housing prices to rise is for demand to rise by more than supply rises.

Our point is that for a correct explanation, we do not need complete information. We do not need to know what is happening or has happened to every variable that can affect the demand for or the supply of houses. We need only *some* information. With only some information, we can logically deduce the correct explanation.

IF YOU'RE SO SMART, THEN WHY AREN'T YOU RICH?

Almost every economist in every college and university in the country can give you an explanation of the Great Depression. Not every economist living at the time of the Great Depression predicted it, though. Similarly, almost every economist can give you an explanation for the stock market crash of 1987, but some of these same economists lost a lot of money in the crash of 1987. Of course, we could give many more such examples. These examples provide us with rough anecdotal evidence that it is harder to predict than to explain.

The difficulty of predicting economic events should help you understand why economists are not necessarily rich. A person who majors in economics in college and then obtains a Ph.D. in economics knows a lot about interest rates, economic growth, stock prices, money, unemployment, and so on. But this knowledge does not guarantee that he or she will be able to consistently predict upcoming economic events accurately. Remember, an incredible amount of information is needed to make accurate predictions consistently, and most economists do not have all this information. If an economist did have all the necessary information (and we assume understood economic relationships correctly), then he or she would be rich—very rich, indeed. The economist would be able to predict prices of bonds, stocks, and houses and, therefore, could always buy low and sell high. Do this often enough and you're rich.

WHY YOU WILL ALWAYS MAKE SOME MISTAKES

Why do even careful and thoughtful people sometimes make mistakes? Is it primarily because it is easier to offer correct explanations than to make accurate predictions? Think about what a mistake is. It is the recognition that if you could to do something over again, you would do it differently.

For example, a person buys a car that ends up being a lemon and says, "Buying this car was a real mistake. If I could go back in time, I wouldn't buy this car."

Or consider the person who believes a relationship with another person was a mistake. She says, "I wish I hadn't married John. He turned out to be a different person than I thought he would turn out to be. If I could do things over again, I wouldn't marry John."

The reason even careful and thoughtful people make mistakes—the reason they regret past decisions—is because they do not have complete information when they make their decisions. A person doesn't know everything there is to know about a car when he buys a car. A person doesn't know everything there is to know about a person when she chooses to marry him. People have difficulty predicting accurately because they don't have complete information. Making mistakes is simply a natural consequence of this state of the world.

This does not mean that we can't lower the incidence of mistakes. We can make use of all the information that is available and that is economically feasible to acquire. But even after we have done that, we sometimes will still make mistakes.

What the Economist Thinks

- *Making a correct prediction is more difficult than offering a correct explanation.* The main reason for this has to do with the amount of information needed for each. A person needs more information to make a correct prediction than to give a correct explanation.

- *Even a complete understanding of all economic relationships does not guarantee that someone will be rich.* For example, a person might know that factors *A–D* influence supply and that factors *E–H* influence demand. But in order to predict prices (and thus be able to become rich by buying low and selling high), the person has to know which factors are changing (Are *B* and *G* changing?), by how much (Is *B* doubling and *G* falling by 10 percent?), and what effect this has on relative changes in supply and demand (Is the *B* effect stronger and does it outweigh the *G* effect on demand?). A lot of information is needed to predict prices, and the person probably will not have some of this information.

- *Making mistakes is a function of many factors, but one important factor is incomplete information.*

Questions to Answer

1. What is the difference between a prediction and an explanation? Stated differently, what question are you trying to answer when you make a prediction? What question are you trying to answer when you offer an explanation?

2. What kind of information do you need in order to predict a change in prices—whether the change is in the prices of stocks, bonds, television sets, or houses?

3. The price of good X depends on the demand for and supply of good X. Furthermore, the supply of good X is a function of variables A–E, and the demand for good X is a function of variables F–T. You know how each variable A–T is related to either supply or demand; that is, you know there is an inverse relationship between A and the supply of good X, a direct relationship between variable R and the demand for good X, and so on. Do you have enough information to accurately predict the price of good X on a consistent basis? Why or why not?

4. An economist would probably believe that it is better to make some mistakes than to never make a mistake. Do you agree or disagree with the statement? Explain your answer.

5. Give an example (other than the one used in text) that illustrates that you need less information to offer a correct explanation than to make an accurate prediction.

chapter 6

Did You Really Mean to Pay for That?

A friend is having problems and you want to help. Your friend is unemployed and has very little money. Unfortunately, he is also an alcoholic. This month he has $500 to spend. He can do various things with the $500: pay his rent, buy food, buy clothes, buy liquor, and so on. Let's suppose that his priorities are to pay his rent first, then buy food, next buy clothes, and then buy liquor. If he doesn't have enough money for everything, then he eliminates items beginning at the bottom of his list. In other words, the first item he would eliminate if he does not have enough money is buying liquor.

Well, at least your friend has his priorities straight. He is not willing to buy liquor instead of food, and he is not willing to buy liquor instead of paying his rent. Perhaps you believe that a person who has his priorities straight and who needs help should receive some help. What is paradoxical, though, is that help may not always have the intended effect.

To illustrate, suppose your friend has to pay $300 in rent, $150 for food, and $50 for clothes this month. At these dollar amounts, his entire $500 will be spent on rent, food, and clothes. He will have no money left to buy liquor. However, you choose this month to help your friend, and so you give him $200. You tell him to use the money to buy more food or to buy a few more clothes or simply to keep the money for an emergency. But instead of buying more food or more clothes or saving for an emergency, your friend may prefer to buy liquor. True, buying liquor is lower on his list of priorities than paying $300 in rent, buying $150 worth of food, and buying $50 worth of clothes, but it may be higher than buying more food or more clothes or saving for an emergency.

What might your friend do with $700 instead of $500? It is likely that he will pay his rent ($300), buy food ($150), buy clothes ($50), and spend the remaining $200 on liquor. In other words, your charitable act of giving your friend $200 has given him the chance to buy liquor that he would not have purchased otherwise. Your intentions were good; you wanted to help your friend. But unfortunately, your action had an effect that you did not intend: it made it possible for your friend to buy liquor. From your perspective, your intention to make your friend better off ended up making him worse off.

WHY NOT GIVE GOODS INSTEAD OF MONEY?

If you can't make your friend better off by giving him $200 (he may just spend it on liquor), then why not give your friend goods instead of money? That is, instead of giving your friend $200 and telling him to spend it on food or clothes, you could simply buy your friend $200 worth of food and clothes.

Does giving goods (food and clothes) instead of money solve the problem? Is this the way for the charitable to make sure that their gifts are used in ways they want them to be used? Not necessarily.

To illustrate, again suppose that your friend plans to spend his $500 on food, clothes, and rent. He will not have any money left to buy liquor. Then, before he has fully spent his $500, you give him $200 worth of food and clothes. To keep things simple, we will assume that you give him $150 worth of food and $50 worth of clothes. Now that you have given him the $200 worth of food and clothes that he would have bought, he doesn't have to buy $200 worth of food and clothes. In other words, he spends $300 (of his $500) on rent, you buy him $200 worth of food and clothes, and he has $200 (of his $500) to spend on anything he wants. It is as if you had simply handed him $200 cash. If he spends his $200 on liquor, then your $200 gift of food and clothes again would have had an unintended effect. It would have made it possible for him to buy liquor.

We conclude that whether you give your friend $200 cash or $200 worth of food and clothes, you make it possible for him to buy liquor that he would not have purchased otherwise.

LET'S CHANGE THE EXAMPLE AND SEE IF WE GET DIFFERENT RESULTS

For those who now think that it is impossible to obtain your objectives through giving, think again. A slight change in the example will bring about different results. Instead of your friend having $500 for the month, suppose he has only $300. You will remember that when he had $500, he planned to spend $300 on rent, $150 on food, and $50 on clothes. With $300 instead of $500, your friend cannot pay his rent and buy food and clothes too. If you give your friend $200, he will be able to pay his rent and buy food and clothes. But, he will not have enough money to buy liquor. In this case, your $200, if you choose to give it, will be used in a way that you deem acceptable.

What is the lesson? Simply, that your $200 gift will be used for whatever is next on your friend's list that he cannot purchase without you. When he had enough money to pay rent and buy food and clothes, your money was used for what was next on his list—buying liquor. But when he had enough money only to pay rent, your money was used to buy food and clothes because these items were next on his list. The general principle is that the gift giver makes it possible for the gift recipient to do whatever is next on his or her "to do" list. If the next thing on the "to do" list is to buy a computer, then the gift giver makes it possible for the recipient to buy a computer. If the next thing on the "to do" list is to buy illegal drugs, then the gift giver makes it possible for the recipient to buy illegal drugs.

WHY PROFESSORS MIGHT SAY NO TO REVIEW SESSIONS

Three days before an economics test, a student raises his hand and asks the professor, "Will you have a review session before the test?" The professor says, "No." At this point, the students in the class might think that the professor is being selfish with her time and doesn't care how her students do on the test. This might be true. Or, it might be far from the truth.

The review session can be seen by the students as something they don't expect but would like to have. In other words, it can be viewed as a gift of sorts. But the professor may not want to give the gift of a review session because she knows that gifts sometimes cannot be given the way the gift giver prefers.

To illustrate, suppose the average student will study four hours for the test if the professor does not give a review session but will study only two hours if the professor does give a review session. So from the student's perspective, the review session means that he does not have to study as long to get a certain grade. In short, what the professor gives (as a gift) to the student when she holds a review session is time. Specifically, she gives the student two hours of time.

What will the student do with those two hours of time? He will do whatever is next on his "to do" list. If the next thing on his list is "read a classic book," then that is the gift given to the student. If the next thing on his list is "drink beer and watch television," then that is the gift given to the student.

When the professor refuses to hold a review session, it is not clear whether she is selfish with her time and doesn't care how her students do on the test or whether she wants to prevent her students from watching as much television and drinking as much beer.

- *If you give money to a person and ask him to use the money to buy X, then even if he buys X, you might have paid for something other than X.* For example, suppose a person has the following "to do" list: (1) Buy X for $100, (2) buy Y for $100, and (3) buy Z for $100. The person has only $100 to spend. You give the person $100 and ask him to use it to buy X. He does. Now he has $100 to spend on Y. It is just as correct to say that your money was used to buy Y as to say it was used to buy X.

- *Giving goods instead of cash is no guarantee that your gift won't make it possible for the recipient to purchase something you would have preferred she not purchase.* For example, suppose a person has $100 and the same "to do" list as above. You know the person has $100, but you do not know the priorities of her "to do" list. In other words, you do not know that X is preferred to Y and that Y is preferred to Z. You want to make sure that the person consumes X, and you prefer that she not consume Y. So, you purchase X for her. You have made sure she will consume X (she would have done so anyway because X was at the top of her list), but you have also made it possible for her to purchase and consume Y. Giving the person good X had the same effect as giving her $100 and telling her to purchase Y.

Questions to Answer

1. Why do people give to religious organizations and not to street gangs? (Hint: Consider each entity's "to do" list.)

2. A multimillionaire gives $5 million to a university with specific orders to use the money to build a new dormitory. The university complies with her orders. Did she pay for the dormitory? Explain your answer.

3. Smith gives away about $10 million a year. When he makes a charitable contribution, he specifies how the money is to be spent. The people and organizations to which he has given any money always have complied with his wishes. One day, Smith realizes that the millions of dollars he has given away in the past might have made some things possible that he would prefer not to have made possible. Because he can no longer be sure that his money will be used exactly as he wants, Smith decides to reduce his gift giving. He decides to give away only $1 million a year. In short, his newfound knowledge has had the effect of reducing his charitable giving. Do you see this as desirable or undesirable? Explain your answer.

4. All other things being equal, who would be more charitable: the person who doesn't care what is on a gift recipient's "to do" list or the person who does care? Explain your answer.

5. It is better to give than to receive. Comment.

chapter 7

Is the Grass Really Greener on the Other Side of the Fence?

People often make comparisons in their daily lives. They compare their house with other houses in their neighborhood. They compare their car with other cars on the road. They compare their educational level with that of other people they meet.

After making a comparison, you have some idea of how you stand in relation to others. You might think your car is older and smaller than the cars of the people you know. Or you might think you are better educated than the majority of your friends and acquaintances. When a comparison works against you, there is a natural inclination to think that someone else is doing better than you. You might think he or she has a bigger and better house, for example. You might think, "The grass is greener on the other side of the fence." But is it really?

Economists know that oftentimes the grass is not greener on the other side of the fence. It only seems so because some factor has been ignored. To illustrate this point, we discuss stocks, houses, and jobs.

WHICH STOCK IS BETTER?

Suppose that companies A and B originally issued two stocks, A and B, respectively. Currently, each stock is selling for $100 a share and has an expected return of 10 percent.

So, we have two numbers for each stock—a share price and an expected return. We divide the first by the second and call the result the price-to-expected return ratio. The price of stock A is $100 and its expected return is 10 percent, so the price-to-expected return ratio for stock A is 100 divided by 10, or 10 (to simplify, we drop the dollar and percent signs). The price-to-expected return ratio for stock B is also 10.

Suppose now that you and others learn something new about the companies that originally issued stocks A and B. You learn that company A is on the brink of producing a new product that will revolutionize the industry and that company B is likely to soon lose a costly lawsuit. This news will likely change your perception of the expected return on each stock. You will probably adjust the expected return for stock *A* upward and the expected return for stock *B* downward. Let's say the expected return for stock *A* rises to 15 percent and the expected return for stock *B* falls to 5 percent. Thus, at the current price of $100, the price-to-expected return ratio is now 6.67 for stock *A* and 20 for stock *B*.

Will the change in expected returns affect the prices of the two stocks? It certainly will. People will pay more for a stock they think will offer a higher return, and they will pay less for a stock they think will offer a lower return. The price of stock *A* will rise and the price of stock *B* will fall.

The price adjustment for each stock will stop at some point. A reasonable guess is that this will happen when the price of stock *A* rises to $150 and the price of stock *B* falls to $50. Why are the new prices of $150 for stock *A* and $50 for stock *B* reasonable? Because the price rise in stock *A* and the price decline in stock *B* will continue until neither stock is considered to be "better" or "worse" than the other. If nothing else has happened in the economy except a change in the fortunes of the two companies, this will occur when the price-to-expected return ratio is the same for the two stocks and equal to 10. The new price of stock *A* ($150) divided by its new expected return (15 percent) gives a price-to-expected return ratio of 10; the new price of stock *B* ($50) divided by its new expected return (5 percent) also gives a price-to-expected return ratio of 10. The same price-to-expected return ratio means that the stocks are equally good or equally bad.

LET'S SUMMARIZE OUR ANALYSIS

Before we continue, let's identify the key components of the stock prices example. Doing this will help you understand how economists think and how they analyze a situation.

- We started with two stocks that were, in a sense, equal. They sold for the same price and offered the same expected return.

- Then we changed the situation so that the stocks would no longer be equal. Specifically, we described a situation in which the expected return for stock *A* would rise and the expected return for stock *B* would fall.

- At this point, we needed to make an assumption about how people would respond to the difference in the expected returns of the two stocks. The economist's assumption is that people will seek the highest return. Based on this assumption, we said that people would start selling stock *B* and buying stock *A*.

- Finally, we thought it reasonable to assume that the process of selling stock *B* and buying stock *A* would stop at some point. But at what stock prices would the process stop?

- To answer the question, we returned to the original price-to-expected return ratio. If a price-to-expected return ratio of 10 prevailed originally and nothing changed in the economy except the economic fortunes of the two companies, then we could reasonably assume that the old ratio would still prevail. The process of price adjustment would stop, then, when the two companies had the same, and original, price-to-expected return ratio. In other words, neither stock could be considered to have an advantage in price or expected return.

In general terms, we (1) started with two things being equal, (2) made them unequal, (3) made an assumption about how people would react to an inequality, (4) described their actions, and (5) explained how and why the process would end.

Now Let's Look at House Prices

Houses are a lot like stocks, and the people who buy stocks are some of the same people who buy houses.

Just as there are two stocks in our earlier example, suppose there are two houses. The houses are identical in every way (size, floor plan, price, and so on) except that one is in San Diego, California, and the other is in Buffalo, New York. For those who do not know either city well, San Diego has an exceptionally good climate all year round and Buffalo has exceptionally cold and fierce winters.

Will the difference in climates make a difference in housing prices? (Did the difference in expected returns make a difference in stock prices?) Before we begin our analysis of house prices, we need to make this example perfectly analogous to the stock prices example and, therefore, understandable in terms of that example.

Imagine that the two houses are initially located next to each other in some city other than San Diego or Buffalo, sell for the same price, and provide the same utility (measured in utils) to their owners. The price of each is $150,000, and each house provides 100,000 utils. If we compute the utils-to-price ratio (utils are in the numerator and price is in the denominator), or util return, we get 0.67 for each house.

Now imagine that with a snap of our fingers, we transport one house to San Diego and one house to Buffalo. Furthermore, we assume that the climate is better in San Diego and worse in Buffalo than in the city from which the houses were transported.

Because of the climate differences, the utility goes up for the San Diego house and down for the Buffalo house. Let's say it rises to 200,000 utils in San Diego and falls to 75,000 utils in Buffalo. At the current price of $150,000 for each house, the util return for the San Diego house rises to 1.3 and the util return for the Buffalo house falls to 0.50.

What will happen next? Just as in the stock prices example, we assume that people search out the highest return. A higher return (more utility per dollar) exists in San Diego than in Buffalo. People will want to sell "Buffalo stock" (move away from Buffalo) and buy "San Diego stock" (move to San Diego). As people move from Buffalo to San Diego, house prices rise in San Diego and fall in Buffalo.

The process of price adjustment will continue until the util return for a house in San Diego is equal to the util return for a house in Buffalo and each is equal to the original util return of 0.67. Thus, prices will adjust until the price of the San Diego house rises from $150,000 to $300,000 and the price of the Buffalo house falls from $150,000 to $112,500.

Which Is the "Greener" Side of the Fence?

When all price adjustments have been made, the San Diego house is no better or worse than the Buffalo house. Both houses offer the same util return. What you don't have in San Diego—low house prices—you do have in Buffalo. And what you don't have in Buffalo—a good climate—you do have in San Diego.

Or look at it this way: What initially gave the San Diego house the edge over the Buffalo house (good climate) now comes with a price—$150,000 for the good climate in San Diego. In other words, the good climate in San Diego has a $150,000 "tax" attached to it. (The person living in San Diego can think of paying $150,000 for the house and $150,000 for the good climate for a total of $300,000.) For the Buffalo house, the bad climate now comes with a "subsidy" of $37,500. Because of the bad climate, the house price is lower. (The person living in Buffalo can think of paying $150,000 for the house and then getting $37,500 returned because of the bad climate in Buffalo.)

So, is it really greener on the other side of the fence? The Buffalo resident sits in his house in the middle of January and envies the San Diego resident basking in the sun. To the Buffalo resident, it looks "greener" in San Diego. The San Diego resident, paying his large mortgage payments, hears about house prices in Buffalo. He envies the Buffalo resident who paid much less for the same house that he has. To the San Diego resident, it looks "greener" in Buffalo.

When we consider only climate, San Diego is "greener"; when we consider only house prices, Buffalo is "greener." But when we consider *both* climate and house prices at the same time (which we need to do to get an accurate picture), one city is as "green" as the other.

A Pinch of Reality

Having read this far, many people say something like the following: "It's easy to sell one stock and buy another. I can simply call my broker, tell her to sell stock *B* and buy stock *A*, and the process is over in a matter of minutes. I don't need much time to seek out the highest return when dealing with stocks. But selling and buying houses isn't so easy. I can't easily move from Buffalo to San Diego simply because the util return is higher in San Diego than it is in Buffalo. If people can't easily move to the city with the higher util return, then the util return for houses in the two cities is never likely to be the same. In other words, because of the relative immobility of people, the adjustment in prices described in the stock prices example isn't likely to occur for houses. And if the price adjustment doesn't occur, then one place actually could be 'greener' than another."

A person who makes these statements has correctly identified the fact that moving out of some things (such as stocks) is easier than moving out of other things (such as houses). The person has gone on to conclude that because of this difference in ease of movement, price and return would not adjust the way we have described.

There is merit to this argument. Economists make the same point when they say that the **transaction costs** of various activities are different. Certainly, the transaction costs of selling one stock and buying another are much less than the transaction costs of selling a house in one city, moving to another city, and buying another house. An important economic principle states that the higher the transaction costs of doing something, the less likely that thing will be done. In short, we should witness in the real world that people will be much more likely to buy and sell stocks in their search for the highest stock return than they will be to buy and sell houses, and move, in their search for the highest house-and-location return.

But the conclusion that no stock is "greener" than any other stock but that houses in some locations are "greener" than other houses in other locations is not valid. We simply have to include the transaction costs component in the analysis.

To illustrate, we return to the housing example. If transaction costs were zero, the San Diego house price would rise from $150,000 to $300,000 and the Buffalo house price would fall from $150,000 to $112,500. But in this situation, transaction costs are not zero. Suppose transaction costs are $33,000. In other words, the cost of selling a house, moving to another city, and buying a house is $33,000. This transaction cost will not be overlooked by Buffalo residents. They are not likely to move from Buffalo to San Diego in search of the initially higher util return in San Diego if their expected benefits are not more than $33,000. Expected benefits of $33,000 or less would keep them in Buffalo.

When transaction costs are positive, the price of houses in San Diego will not rise quite as high as when transaction costs are zero. And as discussed above, the price of houses in Buffalo will not fall quite as low as when transaction costs are zero. But when transaction costs are factored in—and they are real costs that need to be considered—one city is as "green" as the other.

ARE PHYSICIANS REALLY RICH?

There are many different types of physicians—family physicians, internists, surgeons, gastroenterologists, urologists, pediatricians, and so on. The average physician's salary is about $190,000 a year. The average surgeon's salary is higher, about $310,000; and the average pediatrician's salary is lower, about $126,000. However, regardless of the type of physician, physicians are some of the top income earners in the country.

Some people tend to think that the more income you earn, the better off you are. But an economist doesn't look at things this way. She realizes that a certain amount of time and effort is required to earn an income. For an economist, earning $100,000 annually by working 20 hours a week and exerting very little effort is not the same as earning $100,000 annually by working 70 hours a week and exerting a lot of effort under very stressful conditions.

With this in mind, think of a physician's salary. Most physicians have to do quite a lot to obtain their relatively high salaries. The average physician works 52 hours and sees about 110 patients a week. A physician also works under stressful conditions, largely due to the possible result of making an error. A mistake by a physician can cause an individual a great deal of pain or even cause a person's death. When physicians' salaries are adjusted for the long hours and stressful work, are physicians really paid much better than the average person?

We can analyze this situation in much the same way that we analyzed stock prices and house prices. Suppose a physician earns $190,000 a year and an accountant earns $60,000 a year. Each has to work some number of hours a week, exert a certain amount of effort, and experience some amount of stress to earn his or her income. Let's use the term "factor X" to refer to the total amount of hours, effort, and frustration. If we assume factor X is 200 for physicians and 100 for accountants, then the salary-to-X ratio is 950 for a physician and 600 for an accountant. The physician earns more income per one unit of factor X than does the accountant. In other words, the return for being a physician is higher than the return for being an accountant.

Again, the economist assumes that people search out the highest return. How will people seek the highest return in this situation? Young people who are debating whether to become physicians or accountants will decide in favor of becoming physicians. Labor will reallocate itself toward medicine and away from accounting. This will lower physicians' salaries and raise accountants' salaries. (For those who think physicians' salaries never go down, the evidence states otherwise. Physicians' salaries have gone down in recent years, especially for certain specialties.)

How far will physicians' salaries fall and accountants' salaries rise? Salaries will adjust until the salary-to-factor X ratio is the same for the two professions. In the end, for the "average" person, being a physician will be no better or worse than being an accountant.

TRYING TO STOP THE ADJUSTMENT PROCESS

The results we are getting—no stock is better or worse than any other, San Diego is as "green" as Buffalo, and being a physician is no better or worse than being an accountant—depend on the process of adjustment running through to completion. For example, if the return for being a physician is greater than the return for being an accountant and people move into the medical field as a result, they must keep moving into the medical field until there is no further reason to move.

But suppose you were a physician and saw all these new entrants flowing into the medical field pipeline. You could predict the future: plenty of competition for your services. And with the additional competition, your salary might fall or might not rise as fast as it would otherwise.

You might be inclined to try to stop the process of adjustment. You might say that we don't need more physicians in the United States or that medical costs will rise if there are too many physicians. You would have a monetary incentive to try to keep the higher return you are earning from dwindling to the return earned in other professions. Whether you are successful in stopping the adjustment process has little to do with how productive you are or how well you practice medicine. It has much to do with how politically astute and savvy you are.

- *No matter what the activity—buying and selling stocks, choosing a profession, or buying and selling houses—people will seek the highest return.* The search for the highest return ends when returns have been equalized. When returns have been equalized, it is not greener on one side of the fence than it is on the other side.

- *The returns-equalizing process can only take place if resources can be shifted out of one activity and into another.*

- *If people currently receive the highest return, they may try to prevent competition from others seeking the high return.* In short, people search out and try to keep the highest return.

Questions to Answer

1. We identify three ratios in this chapter: the price-to-expected return ratio (for stock prices), the utils-to-price ratio (for housing prices), and the salary-to-X ratio (for various professions). The various ratios play an important part in our analysis. The process of adjustment in response to an initially higher return in one particular area ends when specific ratios return to their original levels. Give anecdotal evidence to attest that people act as if they are trying to reestablish certain original ratios.

2. If it is no better or worse to own a house in San Diego than in Buffalo, own stock A instead of stock B, and work as a physician or as an accountant, then do you think it also follows that it is no better or worse to marry person X than to marry person Y? Explain your answer.

3. Economists believe that people search out and try to keep the highest return. In this chapter, the "people search out the highest return" part of the statement explains how returns on stocks become equalized. The "people try to keep the highest return" part of the statement is discussed in the chapter in describing why physicians, or any other professional group, might argue against others moving into their ranks if they thought the increased supply of competitors would diminish their current high return. Identify two examples where "people search out the highest return" explains something other than that which is explained in this chapter.

4. You will pay the same price for a Snickers bar whether you purchase it in southern California or central Michigan. You will pay a much higher price for a house in southern California than for an identical house in central Michigan. Why the difference between candy bars and houses?

5. There is a Buddhist saying that suffering comes when we strive for too much. If this is true, then how does the realization that "things aren't always greener on the other side of the fence" reduce suffering?

chapter 8

Why There Will Always Be Lies and Liars

How do you define a lie? The dictionary defines a lie as a statement that one knows to be false. For example, suppose Brown asks Thompson if he will drive her to the airport tomorrow morning at 8 o'clock. Thompson says that he will. But at the time he tells Brown that he will drive her to the airport, Thompson knows that he will not do so. According to the dictionary definition of a lie, Thompson is telling Brown a lie. He is making a statement that he knows is false.

Now suppose that when Thompson says he will drive Brown to the airport the next morning at 8 o'clock, he has every intention of doing so. When the next day comes, however, and Thompson has to actually drive Brown to the airport, he decides not to do so because it seems like too much of an effort. In this case, according to the dictionary definition of a lie, Thompson has *not* lied to Brown. At the time he told Brown he would drive her to the airport, he fully intended to do it. It was only later, when the time to drive Brown to the airport arrived, that Thompson reassessed the situation and decided not to drive her to the airport.

Of course from Brown's perspective, whether Thompson told a lie or simply reassessed the situation doesn't really matter. In either case, the effect on Brown is the same—she doesn't have a ride to the airport.

For our purposes, we will define a lie in terms of its effect and not, as is the case with the dictionary definition of a lie, in terms of its intent. In the dictionary definition of a lie, the intent is to deceive. In our definition of a lie, the effect is the same as if one had intended to deceive. Specifically, we define a lie as a statement that specifies certain behavior that is voluntarily not carried out. Whether the person making the statement knew or did not know the behavior would not be carried out is not the issue. So, according to our definition, a lie has been told when there is a difference between what a person says he will do and what he chooses to do. If he says he will do X but chooses instead to do Y, then he has told a lie, irrespective of what his intent was when he said he would do X.

We Lie to Ourselves All the Time

On Saturday, Joann gets on the scale and doesn't like what she sees. She would like to lose about 10 pounds. She promises herself that she will exercise four times a week for three months and cut out sweets for a month. She immediately gets off the scale and goes for a jog. At work on Monday, she turns down the cookies that a coworker offers her.

Joann finds it a little harder to keep her promise the next day. To exercise four times a week, she will have to exercise either before she goes to work, which will require getting up earlier than usual, or after she gets home from work, which will cut out some of her relaxation time at home. She decides to do the former. On Monday night, she sets the alarm clock for thirty minutes earlier than usual. When the buzzer sounds Tuesday morning, she rolls over and turns it off. She tells herself that she *should* get up and go for a jog, but she ends up not doing so. Instead, she rolls over and sleeps a little longer. Then at work that afternoon, someone offers Joann some chocolate candy. She says she *shouldn't* eat any, but she does anyway. This behavior continues much the same way day after day. A month passes during which Joann has exercised only one time and turned down sweets only two out of ten times.

So, Joann said she was going to exercise four times a week for three months and cut out sweets for a month, but she hasn't done either. In other words, she lied to herself. But why did she lie? As odd as it may sound, she lied because it is relatively easier to say something than to do that something. It is easy for someone to say she is going to exercise and cut out sweets. All she has to do is open her mouth and utter the words. But to actually exercise and stop eating sweets takes willpower and determination.

Why Do People Lie?

An economist would say that the costs of *saying something* are much lower than the costs of *doing something* and that is why we say we will do many more things than we end up doing. It is as if saying that we will exercise and cut out sweets costs 1 cent and actually exercising and turning down sweets costs $100. Or it is as if saying that we will drive someone to the airport costs 1 cent and actually driving the person to the airport costs $100. Our words are cheap and our actions are expensive. Is it any wonder then that we sometimes don't do the things that we say we're going to do?

Lying is really just a reflection of the law of demand. The law of demand states that as the price of a good falls, the quantity demanded rises, and as the price of a good rises, the quantity demanded falls, *ceteris paribus.* The "price" of saying we are going to exercise is relatively low, so we say it often. But the "price" of actually exercising is relatively high, so we don't exercise often. In other words, because we consume more of what is cheap and less of what is expensive, there is a difference between what we say we will do and what we do. Stated differently, because it is relatively cheaper to say we will do *X* than it is to do *X*, we end up saying things that we don't do. We lie.

To not lie, one of two things would have to happen. Either the price of saying things and doing things would have to be the same (words would no longer be cheaper than actions) or our behavior would have to change so that it was no longer consistent with the law of demand. Neither of these things is likely to happen, and therefore, there will always be lies and liars.

WHAT ARE PEOPLE MOST LIKELY TO LIE ABOUT?

Let's summarize our discussion so far: The cost of saying you will do something is lower than the cost of doing what you said you would do, and this difference in costs explains why we say many things we end up not doing. That is, this difference in costs explains why we lie to ourselves and to others.

But people do not lie equally about everything. They tell more lies about some things than about other things. When are people least likely to lie? When are they most likely to lie?

Before answering these questions, let's consider two situations. In situation 1, the cost of saying you will do *X* is $1 and the cost of doing *X* is $5. In situation 2, the cost of saying you will do *Y* is $1 and the cost of doing *Y* is $100. Will you be more likely to lie about doing *X* or *Y*? An economist would say that you would be more likely to lie about doing *Y*. The reason is that while the cost of your saying you will do *X* and *Y* is the same ($1), the cost of actually doing *Y* is higher than the cost of actually doing *X*.

The general principle is that people will tell more lies the greater the gap between the cost of saying something and the cost of doing it. More lies will be told if the gap is $99, which is the case with *Y*, than if the gap is $4, which is the case with *X*.

For example, Smith tells you he will call you at 8 p.m.; Jones tells you he will always be your friend, he will always be there for you, and he will always do everything in his power to make sure you are happy. Which person is more likely to be telling a lie? The answer is Jones. While the cost to each person of saying what he says is about the same, the cost of making a call at 8 p.m. is much less than the cost of doing everything to make sure you are happy and so on.

REDUCING THE NUMBER OF LIES

This chapter has discussed why there will always be lies and liars and why lies are more likely to be told about those things where the gap between the cost of saying something and the cost of doing that something is large rather than small. Now, we consider the total number of lies that people will tell.

Some things cannot be measured but nevertheless exist. One of those things is the number of lies told per 100,000 persons. Let's call the number of lies per 100,000 persons the lie rate. If 1,000 lies are told (each day) for every 100,000 persons, then the lie rate is 0.01. The lie rate is likely to fluctuate. It will rise and fall. For instance, the lie rate might be higher or lower today than it was, say, during the Civil War.

What might cause the lie rate to rise and fall? For example, if the lie rate is higher today than it was during the Civil War or during the 1950s or at any other time, then what has caused it to be higher? Why are we becoming a country of increasingly more liars?

An economist would say that people will tell more lies when lies are cheap and will tell fewer lies when lies are expensive. For example, people will tell more lies to their friends than to a judge in a courtroom. The cost of lying to a judge is relatively high compared to the cost of lying to friends. Friends can't put people in jail for the lies they tell, but a judge can.

Or consider that people will tell fewer lies when there is a social stigma attached to lying and will tell more lies when there isn't. If when people told lies, other people castigated and denounced them, then people wouldn't tell as many lies as if others simply accepted the lies with a shrug.

To illustrate, suppose your friend Bob promises to pick you up at 3 p.m., ten minutes after your last class. For no good reason, he arrives an hour late. As you open the door to the car, he says that he is sorry he is late. Suppose you respond, "No problem. These things happen." Or, suppose you say instead, "You are inconsiderate and rude for making me wait an hour. I know we had plans to hang out together, but I don't feel like being around such a rude person. I'm going to take the bus home. Goodbye."

The cost of Bob's lie is higher (to him) when you call him inconsiderate and rude and say goodbye than when you simply shrug off his lateness. Is his future behavior likely to be the same no matter which response you offer? An economist would say no. He would predict that the higher the cost (to Bob) of lying (to you), the less likely Bob will lie. In other words, we have the ability to increase or decrease the number of lies that people tell us by decreasing or increasing the cost of their lies to them.

- *Because the cost of saying something is less than the cost of doing that something, there will always be a difference between what people say they will do and what they actually do.*

- *The greater the gap between the cost of saying something and the cost of doing something, the more likely a person will not do what she said she would do.*

Questions to Answer

1. Jackie and Karen promise to exercise four times a week. Jackie keeps the promise and Karen does not. Given the difference in the cost of saying something and doing it—which holds equally for the two women—why didn't they exhibit the same behavior?

2. In this chapter, we made these statements: "An economist would say that the costs of saying something are much less than the costs of doing something and that is why we say we will do many more things than we end up doing. ... Our words are cheap and our actions are expensive. Is it any wonder then that we sometimes don't do the things that we say we're going to do?" These statements identify a difference between the cost of saying something and the cost of doing that something, and then issue a prediction based on this difference. The prediction is that there will be a difference between what we say and what we do. Nothing is ever said about the benefits of saying something relative to the benefits of doing something. Given the prediction stated, what implicit assumption is being made about the benefits of saying something and the benefits of doing something?

3. Why do some people lie more than others?

4. People can lie to themselves and to others. Suppose Jack lies more to himself than to others, Bill lies more to others than to himself, and Vernon lies equally to himself and to others. Assuming that the number of "others" is the same for each person, what explains the difference in behavior?

5. Do you think the lie rate is likely to be higher or lower in a big city than it is in a small town? Explain your answer.

chapter 9

How Things Will Turn Out

Suppose John is watching a television show in the family room of his house. Sherrie, John's sister, walks into the family room and sees what is on television. She asks John if he would mind if she changes the channel. She says there is a show she would like to watch on another channel. (She cannot watch her show on another television set because there is only one television set in the house.) How will things turn out? Will Sherrie get to watch what she wants? Will John continue to watch the show he is currently watching?

Or, consider another situation. Suppose David, who is married to Alice, wants a divorce. Alice does not want a divorce. How will things turn out? Will the couple get a divorce?

You may think you don't have enough information to decide how things will turn out in either of these situations. For example, you may think you need to know the state in which David and Alice reside and its divorce laws. Does their state grant a divorce even if only one person wants the divorce, or do both persons in the marriage have to agree to a divorce?

But information is not what you need to find out how things will turn out. You need a way of looking at the world. You need to think like an economist.

THE ECONOMIST'S MINDSET

An economist can answer numerous questions without obtaining information. For example, an economist can tell you in broad terms what will happen in both the television and the divorce situations.

Let's look first at the television situation. John is watching a show on television and Sherrie wants to change the channel. In other words, John has something that Sherrie wants. Have you ever wanted something that someone else had? How did you obtain what you wanted?

An economist would say that entering into a trade is one of the key ways to get what you want from someone. The simplest kind of trade is a monetary trade.

For example, suppose you want a book about Thomas Jefferson, the third President of the United States. You go to your local bookstore, look in the biography section, find a book about Jefferson, and skim through it. You decide you want the book. The price of the book is $23.95. By posting this price on the book, the bookstore owner is telling you what you have to give her to get what you want. You give her $23.95, and she will gladly give you the book. She will even throw in a smile for free. In short, you often get what you want by buying it from someone who has it. (As an aside, do you think an economist would say the smile is free? Would the price of the book be lower if the bookseller did not smile?)

Now let's consider a nonmonetary trade. Suppose you're in your last class of the day. You're anxious to get home after class, but your car is in the shop. A classmate who is sitting next to you has a car and is planning on leaving campus after class. You want something from him: you want him to give you a ride home after class. How do you get what you want? You could, very subtly, enter into a trade with him. You might say, "Joe, could give me a ride home? My car is in the shop. Maybe on the way home I can tell you what you missed in class when you were absent last week." The nature of the trade is that you will tell Joe what happened in class in return for a ride home.

Thus by trading, you can sometimes get what you want but do not have; that is, you can offer either money or something else to the person who has what you want. With this in mind, let's return to the television situation. Sherrie might get what she wants by simply offering "to buy" access to the television from John. Whether her offer will be successful or not depends on how much she values getting what she wants relative to how much John values continuing to watch the show he is watching.

To illustrate, let's assume that John values continuing to watch the show he is watching at $10. This means he would be willing to pay $10, or to forfeit receiving $10, to continue watching the show. We assume that Sherrie values watching a different show at $15. This means she would be willing to pay $15, or to forfeit receiving $15, to change the channel. While Sherrie is willing to pay $15 to get what she wants (the right to change the channel), she would prefer to pay less than $15; she would prefer to pay $0. So, with this in mind, she might not offer John anything in exchange for his giving up the television set. She might simply ask, "John, do you mind if I change the channel?" This question translates to, "I don't want to pay you anything for the right to change the channel. Will you accept those terms?"

However, John will not accept those terms because we have assumed that he values watching his show at $10. Then, Sherrie is likely to up the ante. She will offer more than $0. She might offer $2, to which John will say no; then, she might offer $4, to which John will say no. Only when Sherrie offers more than $10 will he say yes. At an offer of, say, $13, John would consider it worthwhile to let Sherrie watch whatever she wants to watch.

People usually criticize our analysis at this point. They often say that brothers and sisters do not usually decide who will determine what is on television by offering to enter into a monetary trade. Economists agree that this isn't usually the way this situation would be resolved. But, then, economists never meant to give the impression that the situation would actually be resolved this way.

Economists talk about money, prices, purchases, and sales to easily and clearly get at the relevant point. The relevant point has to do with trade and value. Trade is the way people get what they want, and value expresses how much they want what they want.

When an economist assumes that John is willing to pay $10 to continue watching his show and Sherrie is willing to pay $15 to change the channel, all the economist is saying is that Sherrie values access to the television set more than John does. After establishing this point, the relevant question then becomes how Sherrie expresses her higher value. She may not do it in money terms, that is, by offering John money to give her the right to change the channel, but she will do it in some way.

For example, she might tell John that she is willing to clean his room if he lets her change the channel, or that she will tell a lie for him if he lets her change the channel, or any of a number of other things. Of course, Sherrie has some limit to what she will do, and the $15 expresses that limit. For example, she might be willing only to tell a cheap lie—"a $15 lie"—if John lets her change the channel.

So with all this as background, let's return to our original questions about John and Sherrie: How will things turn out? Will Sherrie get to watch what she wants? Will John continue to watch the show he is currently watching?

An economist can only tell what will happen in very broad terms. According to an economist, the person who values access to the television more will end up deciding the television channel. In economic terms, a resource (and in this case, the television set is a resource) will end up in the hands of the person who values it more. In our discussion, we have assumed that Sherrie values access to the television more than John does. So, based on our assumption, she ends up with it.

OUR DIVORCE SITUATION

Now let's consider the divorce situation. David wants a divorce and Alice does not. How will things turn out? The layperson almost always thinks that a law will determine whether or not David and Alice will divorce. If the law specifies that a divorce can be granted when only one partner wants the divorce, then in the case of David and Alice, a divorce will be granted. But if the law specifies that both partners must agree to the divorce before it is granted, then in the case of David and Alice, a divorce will not be granted.

But to an economist, the law is irrelevant in this situation. The law is irrelevant because the law will not determine how things will turn out. The law does not determine the outcome. What determines the outcome is the value to David of a divorce relative to the value to Alice of staying married.

To illustrate, suppose the law specifies that both husband and wife must agree to a divorce before it will be granted. Furthermore, assume David values a divorce at $100,000 and Alice values staying married at $70,000. Because David values a divorce more than Alice values staying married, he can effectively buy Alice's consent to a divorce for something more than $70,000 but less than $100,000.

Suppose, instead, we assume Alice values staying married at $100,000 and David values getting a divorce at $70,000. In this case, no matter what the law specifies, there will be no divorce because Alice can effectively buy David's consent to stay married for something more than $70,000 but less than $100,000.

Just as in the television situation, how things turn out in the divorce situation depends on how much one person values what he wants relative to how much another person values what she wants. In both situations, the outcome matches the preference of whoever values more what is wanted.

AN IMPORTANT CONDITION IS NECESSARY TO REACH OUR CONCLUSION

In both the television and the divorce situations, an important condition was necessary to reach the conclusion that the outcome matches the preference of whoever values more what is wanted. This condition is that the costs of negotiating and consummating a trade have to be small or negligible. In economics, these costs are called **transaction costs**. In the two situations discussed, transaction costs were implicitly assumed to be zero. If transaction costs are high, the outcome may be different.

To illustrate, again assume that John values watching his current television show at $10 and Sherrie values watching another television show at $15. Furthermore, assume that the transaction costs are $20 for Sherrie. This means that if Sherrie wants to work out a deal with John to change the channel, she will have to spend $20. Is she likely to do this? Of course she isn't because she wouldn't spend $20 to obtain something that is worth $15. The high transaction costs act as a stumbling block that Sherrie isn't likely to climb over.

How, then, will things turn out if transaction costs are high? In the television situation, John will continue to watch the television show that he is currently watching and Sherrie will not get to change the channel. With high transaction costs, the television set may not end up going to the person who values it more.

What the Economist Thinks

- *People make themselves better off through trade.*

- *High transaction costs are an impediment to trade and, therefore, are an impediment to people making themselves better off.*

- *Resources flow to the person who values them more, given the condition that transaction costs are low or negligible.*

Questions to Answer

1. Stephanie values getting a divorce at $60,000, and Bob values staying married at $130,000. In the state in which they live, a divorce can be granted if only one person wants it. If money does not change hands, how might Bob "buy" Stephanie's consent to stay married and not seek a divorce? In other words, how might Bob pay Stephanie something more than $60,000 (and less than $130,000) without actually handing over any money? (Hint: Is it possible to provide a person with $60,000+ worth of benefits?)

2. Give an example to illustrate that as a result of high transaction costs, resources do not flow to the person who values them more.

3. At the heart of any trade is an agreement: you give me what I want and I will give you what you want. Some trades are more obvious than others because the agreement is clearly stated. For example, when a person goes into a clothing store and sees a jacket priced at $100, the agreement is obvious. The seller is saying to the potential buyer: "Give me $100, and I will give you the jacket." Consider a trade that is not so obvious. Suppose Dan gives Jack a birthday present. To some people this looks like Dan is simply giving Jack a gift. But Dan might expect

something in return for giving Jack a birthday present. He might expect to get a birthday present from Jack. In other words, what Dan is really saying to Jack when he gives him a birthday present is: "I will give you a birthday present today, but I expect to get a birthday present from you in exchange." In other words, what initially appears to be a gift is really one side of a trade. Give three examples of what you think many people (at first glance) would consider a gift, but which is really one side of a trade.

4. Assume a town includes a 30-acre parcel of unused land. On the land are wildflowers, trees, birds, squirrels, and insects. Currently, some of the townspeople go to the land to get away from their everyday lives and just enjoy nature. A developer wants to purchase the land for its market value ($10 million) and to build a hotel and golf course. If the developer does this, many of the trees will be cut, many of the birds will fly away, and many of the wildflowers, squirrels, and insects will die. A local environmental group wants the land to stay as it is. The group is willing to pay no more than $2 million to purchase the land. Because the developer is willing to pay more for the land than the environmental group is willing to pay, does it follow that the land is more valuable as a location for a hotel and golf course than as a place where people can enjoy nature? Explain your answer.

5. One divorce law specifies that as long as one person in a marriage wants a divorce, a divorce will be granted. A second divorce law specifies that before a divorce will be granted, both persons in the marriage must agree to the divorce. Under which divorce law, if either, will there be more divorces? Explain your answer.

chapter 10

What Kinds of Explanations Do Economists Use?

Suppose we learn that women have fewer children in rich countries than they do in poor countries. It is not immediately obvious why this would be the case, so we scratch our heads and think about it for a while.

One explanation might be that women in poor countries have a stronger preference for having children than women in rich countries have. That is, women in both poor and rich countries might like having children; it's just that women in poor countries like having children more than women in rich countries do. This explanation is similar to saying that both John and Bob like chocolate ice cream but John likes it relatively more than Bob does.

Thus, we explain an observation (women have fewer children in rich countries than they do in poor countries) by assuming that women in rich countries don't have as strong a preference for having children as women in poor countries do. In other words, we observe different behavior between women in rich and poor countries because women in rich and poor countries have different degrees of preference for children.

While this type of explanation may sound reasonable, something about it makes us suspicious. Namely, it is almost too easy. To illustrate, suppose this time we observe a difference in the behavior of 18-year-old men and women. Specifically, we observe some 18-year-old men and women decide to attend college and some do not. We ask why this would be the case. If we use the same type of explanation as we used to explain the difference in the behavior of women in rich and poor countries, we'd have to say it's because some 18 year olds have a stronger preference to attend college than others do. Those who really want to attend college end up attending college and those who don't care as much about attending college do not attend college.

Or suppose we observe one person smoking cigarettes and another person not smoking cigarettes. How do we explain this? Using the same type of explanation we have been using, we'd have to say it has something to do with a difference in preferences between the smoker and nonsmoker. Obviously, the smoker has a preference for smoking and the nonsmoker has a preference for not smoking.

Now consider the common denominator in our three examples. In each case, something is explained as being caused by a difference in preferences. Rich women do not have as many children as poor women do because rich and poor women have a different degree of preference for children. Some 18 year olds attend college and some do not because some have a preference for attending college and some do not. Some people smoke cigarettes and some do not because some people have a preference for smoking and some do not.

Economists do not like these types of explanations. They do not like explaining a difference in behavior by saying it is caused by a difference in preferences because this type of explanation can "explain" too many different behaviors. Economists look at things differently. For example, an economist might assume that women in rich and poor countries have exactly the same intensity of preference for having children. Then the economist will look for a difference in the cost to women of having children in the two countries.

Of course, when we use the word "cost" here, we are referring to a woman's opportunity cost of having and raising children. Suppose we measure the time required to have and raise children. Let's assume a woman is pregnant for 9 months and is in delivery for 20 hours. So, 6,500 hours are required to have a child. We assume that an average of at least 4 hours a day for 18 years is required to raise a child properly. This is a total of 26,280 hours. Thus, having and raising a child requires 6,500 hours plus 26,280 hours, or 32,780 hours.

Now when a woman is devoting 32,780 hours to having and raising a child, she cannot be earning income during these hours. Suppose the average woman's wage in a poor country is $3 an hour and the average woman's wage in a rich country is $15 an hour. Thus, the cost for a woman in a poor country to have and raise a child is $98,340, and the cost for a woman in a rich country to have and raise a child is $491,700. In other words, the cost of having and raising a child is 5 times higher in a rich country than in a poor country.

Even if, as we have assumed, rich and poor women have the same preferences for having and raising children and, therefore, derive exactly the same amount of benefits from children, we would predict that women in rich countries will have fewer children than women in poor countries will have because the costs of having and raising children is so much higher (relative to the benefits) in a rich country than in a poor country.

GRAPES IN CALIFORNIA AND NEW YORK

In their book *University Economics,* Armen Alchian and William Allen tell a story that is well-known to economists and clearly exemplifies the economic way of thinking. The story is about grapes that have been grown in California and are then sold in California and New York. Alchian and Allen ask: How does one explain the larger proportion of high quality grapes sold in New York than in California?[1]

Before we tell the story, let's identify the facts. Fact 1: Grapes are grown in California and transported to New York. Fact 2: Various qualities of grapes are grown in California. Following Alchian and Allen, we'll call the higher-quality grapes "choice grapes" and we'll call the lower-quality grapes "standard grapes." Fact 3: New Yorkers buy *relatively more* (not absolutely more) choice grapes than standard grapes.

Now why is this? Could it be because New Yorkers are richer and more discriminating in their grape purchases than Californians are? Could it simply be because New Yorkers have a stronger preference for choice grapes than Californians do? To simply say that New Yorkers have different preferences for grapes than Californians have is really too easy an explanation because this type of explanation can "explain" everything and nothing. Alchian and Allen ask us to ponder on the economic explanation for why New Yorkers buy relatively more choice grapes than Californians do. Here is what they have to say:

"Suppose that grapes grown in California cost 5 cents a pound to ship to New York, whether the grapes are 'choice' or 'standard' (poorer quality), that the production of grapes is 50 percent 'choice' and 50 percent 'standard,' and that in California, the 'choice' grapes sell for 10 cents a pound and the 'standard' for 5 cents a pound (in California, 2 pounds of 'standard' and 1 pound of 'choice' grapes sell for the same price). If grapes are shipped to New York, the shipping costs will raise the cost of 'choice' grapes to 15 cents and of 'standard' grapes to 10 cents. In New York, then, the price of 'choice' grapes is lower, relative to 'standard' grapes (1.5 to 1), than in California (2 to 1). To buy 1 pound of 'choice' grapes in New York would mean a sacrifice of 1.5 pounds of 'standard,' whereas in California it would cost 2 pounds of 'standard.' According to our first law of demand [the higher the price, the lower the rate of consumption], New Yorkers, faced with a lower price of 'choice' relative to 'standard,' will consume *relatively* more 'choice' grapes than Californians. In California, where 'standard' grapes are cheaper relative to 'choice' grapes, a larger fraction of 'standard' grapes should be consumed. And it is so."[2]

---

1 Keep in mind here that we are talking about a higher proportion, not a higher absolute number.

2 *University Economics,* Third Edition, by Armen Alchian and William Allen (Belmont, California, 1972), p. 71.

USE WHAT WORKS OFTEN AND WELL

You may wonder why an economist explains a change in behavior by a change in relative costs instead of by a change in preferences. There are two reasons. First, if you accept that a change in preferences explains a change in behavior, you must then explain why there was a change in preferences. For example, if you accept that Michael has different preferences with respect to choice and standard grapes in California and in New York, then you have to explain why he has different preferences. In short, why does Michael have different preferences in different places? This kind of problem does not arise when an economist explains a change in behavior by a change in relative cost.

The second reason an economist will choose the change-in-relative-cost explanation over the change-in-preference explanation is because the change-in-relative-cost explanation has already proved that it can explain changes in behavior in different settings. In other words, suppose there are currently ten different settings, *A–J*, in which Michael operates. The economist is saying that the change-in-relative-cost explanation already explains changes in Michael's behavior in many if not all of the settings *A–J*, so it is likely to explain Michael's behavior in one more setting too. For example, if the change-in-relative-cost explanation explains why Michael smoked fewer cigarettes per day when he learned that smoking causes cancer and if it explains why Michael increased his long distance phone usage when long distance rates went down, then it probably also explains why he purchases relatively more choice grapes when it is relatively cheaper to do so.

What the Economist Thinks

- *When you want to explain a difference in behavior, do not imme-diately assume that preferences are different.* For example, if you learn that women do not have and raise as many children in rich countries as in poor countries, do not assume that this is because women in poor countries like children relatively more than women in rich countries do. To explain a difference in behavior, first look to see if there is a difference in the relative cost of a factor relevant to behavior.

- *When you want to explain changed behavior, do not immediately assume that preferences have changed.* For example, if Michael buys more choice grapes in New York than in California, do not assume that this is because his preferences for grapes have changed. To explain a change in behavior, first look to see if there is a change in the relative cost of a factor relevant to behavior.

Questions to Answer

1. How would an economist try to explain why the crime rate is higher in the United States than it is in England?

2. Women in the United States can be placed into one of three income groups: low, middle, or high. Which income group of women would an economist predict would have and raise more children? Explain your answer.

3. If four-person families in California live in smaller houses than four-person families in Oklahoma live in, what might explain the difference according to an economist? Explain your answer.

4. The economist argues that a difference in behavior can often be explained by a difference in relative costs. With this in mind, consider Frank and Wendy, who are in the same economics class at college. Each night, Frank studies economics for 90 minutes and Wendy studies economics for 45 minutes. Here are various explanations for the difference in time devoted to studying economics by Frank and Wendy:

   Explanation 1: It is relatively cheaper for Frank to study economics than it is for Wendy because Frank earns $7 an hour and Wendy earns $14 an hour.

   Explanation 2: For economics, Frank needs to spend two minutes to understand what Wendy understands in one minute. So, to study a given amount of information, Frank necessarily has to spend twice as much time as Wendy has to spend.

   Explanation 3: Frank likes economics more than Wendy likes economics and therefore studies it more.

   How would you go about determining which explanation, if any, is correct?

5. In many countries, church membership is down. What might be an economic explanation for this?

chapter 11

Good Things
Can Just Happen

Imagine you live in world where money does not exist—that is, you live in a barter economy. You can get the goods and services you want only by trading the goods and services you have in your possession for the goods and services other people have. Suppose you have apples and want bread. You search for a person who has bread and finally you find him. You offer him ten apples for a loaf of bread. He says that he doesn't want apples. Instead, he wants bananas. So you continue on your way and try to find either (1) a person who has bread and wants to trade it for your apples or (2) a person who has bananas and wants to trade them for your apples, after which you return to the person who has bread and trade the bananas for bread.

Obviously, this type of trading can be very time-consuming. You might need hours, if not days, to find the person who has what you want and wants what you have. What can you do to make your life easier?

Consider that some goods in a barter economy will be more marketable than others: they will be more readily accepted in exchange than other goods. To illustrate, suppose there are ten goods, $A-J$, good G is accepted in 50 percent of all exchanges, and all the other goods are accepted in only 15 percent of all exchanges.

You can make your life easier by accepting good G in exchange *even if you do not want to consume good G*. After you begin accepting good G so that trading is easier for you, the marketability of good G rises (perhaps it will now be accepted in 51 percent of all exchanges). Your acceptance of good G raises the marketability of good G and prompts other people to accept it. After other people begin accepting good G, the marketability of good G rises even further—from 51 percent to 52 percent to 53 percent and so on. Through this process, good G eventually becomes widely accepted for purposes of exchange. In other words, it is accepted in nearly 100 percent of all exchanges. When a good becomes widely accepted for purposes of exchange, economists call it **money**.

WHAT ARE THE BENEFITS OF MONEY?

How is your life better when you live in a money economy than when you live in a barter economy?

In a money economy, you can make trades easier than you can in a barter economy. If you want bread in a money economy, you simply find the person who has bread and offer her money. The person who has bread will not turn down the money, saying that she wants bananas, apples, or cakes instead. She will accept your money and then use that money to get the things she wants.

Also, you will spend much less time trading in a money economy than in a barter economy. If, for example, you need an average of 1 hour to trade for a given good in a barter economy, you might need an average of only 2 minutes to trade for the good in a money economy. If you spend less time trading, then you have more time to do other things (58 minutes more time in this case).

You could use the extra time to work and produce goods and services. If everyone used the extra time this way, the society in which you live would become richer. There would be more goods and services for people to enjoy.

Alternatively, you could use the extra time to simply sit back and enjoy life. In other words, instead of working more, you could simply consume more leisure. If everyone used the time this way, the society in which you live would become richer. Not richer in goods and services, but richer in terms of time for people to simply sit back and enjoy life—read a book, talk to a friend, enjoy a sunset, and so on.

Most likely, some of the extra time acquired by moving from a barter economy to a money economy would be used to produce more goods and services, and some would be used to consume more leisure. The society in which you live would then become richer in goods and services and richer in leisure.

No doubt most people would say this is a good thing. After all, most people say that they would like to have both *more* goods and services and *more* leisure.

MONEY WAS NOT INVENTED

No person, living or dead can take credit for our using money today. No king or queen can take credit, no president or prime minister, no scientist or educator, no one.

What—not who—then deserves credit for the emergence of money and all that money makes possible? If anything, money emerged because of something that lies deep in the heart of most people: self-interest.

Self-interest motivated people in a barter economy to accept the most marketable of all goods (good *G* in our example). Sheer self-interest "created" money. In other words, self-interest is the cause, money is the effect.

Moreover, money is an unintended effect. No one intended money to exist; it simply emerged out of the self-interested actions of people living in a barter economy who tried to make their everyday trades in less time. In conclusion, money is the unintended effect of the self-interested, narrowly focused actions of people living in a barter economy.

What the Economist Thinks

- *Certain things emerge spontaneously, without the conscious efforts of anyone and without a blueprint or a plan.* Sometimes the things that emerge spontaneously end up benefiting individuals. Money is an example.

- *Self-interest is the driving force for many of the good things that occur spontaneously and benefit individuals.* However, self-interest might be the driving force for many of the bad things that happen in life too.

Questions to Answer

1. Money is an institution that emerged spontaneously out of the self-interested actions of individuals living in a barter economy. Generally, money is believed to benefit society. Identify another institution that emerged spontaneously out of the self-interested actions of individuals.

2. In the discussion of the emergence of money, we identify the benefits of using money. Can you identify any costs?

3. Money emerged from the self-interested actions of individuals living in a barter economy. No one invented money. In fact, some people say that money could not have been invented. If someone had proposed that people use *X* or *Y* or *Z* as part of every exchange, they would not have complied. Do you agree or disagree? Explain your answer.

4. Beginning tomorrow, U.S. currency can no longer be printed or minted. Furthermore, all U.S. currency that currently exists has disappeared: no dimes, nickels, $1 notes, $10 notes, and so on. Do you think the U.S. economy will be without money a year from tomorrow? If not, why not? What do your answers indicate about the benefits of using money?

5. Are people more likely to specialize in a money economy or in a barter economy? Explain your answer.

chapter 12

Winners and Losers

Economists often think of people in terms of winners and losers. A winner is a person who has gained utility; a loser is a person who has lost utility.

Economists also often think in terms of the "games" that two or more people play. Economists classify these games as positive-sum games, negative-sum games, and zero-sum games and identify different varieties of the three types of games.

POSITIVE-SUM GAMES

Positive-sum games include two varieties of games: (1) only winners and (2) winners and losers where the winners' winnings are greater than the losers' losses.

Let's look at an example of a positive-sum game in which there are **only winners**. Suppose Smith has a computer and Jones has $2,000 cash. Each person gets the following utils from each good:

Smith: 200 utils from the computer (she has)
800 utils from the $2,000 cash (if she had it)

Jones: 400 utils from the $2,000 cash (he has)
900 utils from the computer (if he had it)

Can Smith and Jones do something to make themselves both better off? Yes, they can trade. Smith gives Jones the computer and in return receives $2,000 in cash. Smith is better off by 600 utils and Jones is better off by 500 utils. Both Smith and Jones are winners.

Now let's consider a positive-sum game in which there are **winners and losers and the winners' winnings are greater than the losers' losses**. Suppose in August, country X practices economic protectionism: it imposes high tariffs on all imported goods. In September, country X reconsiders its position and replaces its protectionist policies with free trade. The move from protectionism to free trade creates winners and losers. The winners are the consumers of country X. They end up paying lower prices both for imported goods and for the domestic goods that compete with the imported goods. The losers include the government and the domestic producers who compete with foreign firms. Domestic producers lose some profits; government loses tariff revenue. Economists have shown mathematically, geometrically, and empirically that the benefits to consumers of moving away from tariffs to free trade outweigh the losses sustained by producers and government. In other words, it is as if consumers win $10 billion and producers and government lose $8 billion by moving from tariffs to free trade.

NEGATIVE-SUM GAMES

Negative-sum games also include two varieties of games: (1) only losers and (2) winners and losers where the losers' losses are greater than the winners' winnings.

First, we look at an example of a negative-sum game in which there are **only losers**. Suppose Smith challenges Jones to a duel and Jones accepts. They count off 20 paces, turn, and fire. When the smoke clears, both Smith and Jones are dead. Both Smith and Jones are losers.

Now let's consider a negative-sum game in which there are **winners and losers and the losers' losses are greater than the winners' winnings**. When a country moves from protectionism to free trade, the winners are the consumers and the losers are the producers and the government. Suppose instead, country Υ has an initial policy of free trade and replaces it with economic protectionism (tariffs). The winners now are the domestic producers and the government; the losers are the consumers. Furthermore, the losers' losses are greater than the winners' winnings. It is as if consumers lose $10 billion and producers and government win $8 billion by moving from free trade to tariffs.

ZERO-SUM GAMES

In a zero-sum game, there are winners and losers and the winners' winnings equal the losers' losses.

For example, suppose five people are sitting at a blackjack table in Las Vegas. The cards are dealt and the bets are made. In the end, what the losers lose, the winners gain. If $400 is lost, then $400 is exactly the dollar amount that is won. As long as all winners and all losers gain or lose as much utility from $1, we have a zero-sum game.

HOW THE ECONOMIST THINKS ABOUT THE VARIOUS GAMES

Suppose life consists of 300 activities. Half of these activities, or 150, can be categorized as two-person activities where it makes sense to speak of positive-sum, negative-sum, or zero-sum games. Furthermore, suppose that of the 150 two-person activities (or games), 60 are positive-sum games, 50 are negative-sum games, and 40 are zero-sum games. The negative-sum games plus the zero-sum games equals 90 games. Thus, the ratio of positive-sum games to negative-sum plus zero-sum games is 67 percent:

$$\frac{\text{Positive-sum games}}{\text{Negative-sum games} + \text{Zero-sum games}} = \frac{60}{90} = 67 \text{ percent}$$

Economists try to think of ways to increase this ratio. Specifically, they try to turn some of the negative-sum and zero-sum games into positive-sum games.

To illustrate, during World War II, the federal government issued ration tickets to control the amount of gasoline, meat, sugar, and so on that each person could buy. Now suppose government officials are trying to decide how the ration-ticket program should be structured. One government official says: "One million pounds of beef are available each month, but consumers want to buy two million pounds each month. Let's issue one ration ticket to each consumer each month and stipulate that with the ration ticket, the person can buy only one-half pound of beef. Furthermore, let's make it illegal for individuals to sell their ration tickets. In other words, if a person doesn't want to use his or her ration ticket, it goes unused."

What would an economist think when hearing these words? An economist would have these thoughts: "This person is proposing a negative-sum game. Suppose Smith and Jones each get one ration ticket but Smith doesn't eat meat and Jones does. Smith would like to sell his ration ticket to Jones, and Jones would like to buy it, but the ration-ticket policy being proposed prevents them from legally doing this. So, both individuals will lose by not being able to buy and sell ration tickets compared to both individuals winning if they could. The choice is between two losers (negative-sum game) or two winners (positive-sum game). What changes a negative-sum game into a positive-sum game is the ability to trade."

In conclusion: Some games are negative-sum games because people can't trade. Often, the way to turn a negative-sum game into a positive-sum game is to introduce the possibility of trade. In other words, an economist often hunts for trades that can be made but aren't being made at the present. For an economist, trade is the bridge that one walks over to get from a negative-sum game to a positive-sum game.

- *Many of life's activities can be categorized as positive-sum, negative-sum, or zero-sum games.*

- *The challenge for an economist is to try to devise ways to turn (at least some subset) of the negative-sum and zero-sum games into positive-sum games.*

Questions and Answers

1. Identify each of the following as a positive-sum game, a negative-sum game, or a zero-sum game:
   a. Jack loses $2 in the lottery.
   b. Two people decide to get married.
   c. Shelly buys 10 books at the bookstore.

2. "One way we can evaluate how good or bad our lives are is to identify what percentage of our days we are winners and what percentage of our days we are losers." Do you agree or disagree with this statement? Explain your answer.

3. "If there is life after death and if any negative-sum games exist in that life, then surely there is no such thing as heaven because heaven is where only positive-sum games are played." Comment.

4. Try to think like an economist by identifying a negative-sum or zero-sum game and then devising a way to turn it into a positive-sum game.

5. Smith has been involved in 100 two-person activities (or games) in life, and 45 of them have been negative-sum games. In 40 of the 45 negative-sum games, her winnings were less than the other person's losses. In the remaining 5 negative-sum games, both she and the other person incurred losses. Jones has been involved in 100 two-person games in life, and 45 of them have been negative-sum games. In 2 of the 45 negative-sum games, his winnings were less than the other person's losses. In 20 of the remaining 43 negative-sum games, his losses were greater than the other person's winnings; and in the other 23 negative-sum games, both he and the other person incurred losses. Do you think Smith is a different type of person than Jones is? If so, in what way? In short, how would you describe each person in terms of personality, behavior, mindset, world view, and so on.

chapter 13

Life Is Just
One Big Real Estate Market

People in the real estate business often talk about a buyers' market or a sellers' market. Generally, a buyers' market means that house buyers have the upper hand in real estate transactions. A sellers' market means that house sellers have the upper hand. If you are trying to sell your house, you want to sell in a sellers' market; if you are trying to buy a house, you want to buy in a buyers' market. You are at a disadvantage in transactions if, as a seller, you sell in a buyers' market or if, as a buyer, you buy in a sellers' market.

Economists describe buyers' and sellers' markets a little more rigorously than the average person does. Economists often speak in terms of supply and demand and thus describe a sellers' market in real estate as one where, at current prices, more people want to buy houses than there are houses available for sale. This means a shortage exists in the real estate market and prices are likely to rise.

Economists describe a buyers' market in real estate as one where, at current prices, there are more houses available for sale than there are people who want to buy houses. This means a surplus exists in the real estate market and prices are likely to fall.

We can also think of buyers' and sellers' markets in terms of the alternatives that buyers and sellers have in each. In a buyers' market, a buyer can choose from many houses. If she doesn't like one house, another house is for sale around the corner. The seller, though, has few alternatives in a buyers' market. If a prospective buyer doesn't buy his house, he might not have many other buyers coming around.

The alternatives are different in a sellers' market. In a sellers' market, a seller can choose from many buyers. If he doesn't like the dollar offer made by a prospective buyer, he can reject the offer and know that another buyer will be on his doorstep tomorrow. A buyer, though, has few alternatives in a sellers' market. If she doesn't buy the house she is considering and doesn't offer (to pay) the seller's price, then she might not have many other houses to buy.

Economists often compute ratios to make relationships clearer and simpler. We can compute the following ratio to analyze the alternatives for buyers and sellers:

$$X = \frac{\text{Buyer's alternatives}}{\text{Seller's alternatives}}$$

Let's say that the buyer has 10 alternatives and the seller has 10 alternatives. So, X is equal to 1. In some sense, the buyer and seller are in an equal position. Suppose the buyer's alternatives rise to 20 and the seller's alternatives remain at 10. Now, X rises to 2. The buyer is in a superior position to the seller because she has more alternatives. Finally, suppose the seller's alternatives rise to 20 and the buyer's alternatives stay constant at 10. Now, X falls to 0.5 and the buyer is in an inferior position to the seller (or the seller is in a superior position to the buyer).

We can say that X represents market power. When X is 1, the person in the numerator of our ratio and the person in the denominator of our ratio have equal market power. No one has the upper hand, so to speak. If X is greater than 1, then the person in the numerator is in the superior position—he or she has the upper hand. And if X is less than 1, then the person in the denominator is in the superior position.

So, in the real estate market, a buyers' market exists if X is greater than 1 (the buyer is in the superior position). A sellers' market exists if X is less than 1.

Buyers' market: $X > 1$
Sellers' market: $X < 1$

WHAT DOES SUPERIOR MARKET POSITION IMPLY?

In the real estate market, buyers and sellers act differently toward each other depending on whether they are in a sellers' market or in a buyers' market. To illustrate, suppose when we do not have either a buyers' or a sellers' market, the seller of a house will usually paint the house and put in new carpet before the new owner takes possession. Furthermore, buyer and seller will usually split escrow fees.

However, in a sellers' market, the seller is not as likely to paint the house and add new carpet, and he is more likely to demand that the buyer pay the full escrow fees. The buyer in this situation will be less likely to request anything of the seller and will probably pay all the fees.

In contrast, in a buyers' market, the seller is more likely to paint the house and add new carpet, and respond to the buyer's request to fix the plumbing too. The buyer might also request that the seller pay the full escrow fees, and the seller is likely to do so.

The layman might put it this way, "In a sellers' market, the seller can get away with more. In a buyers' market, the buyer can get away with more."

WHAT THE ECONOMIST WILL DO AT THIS POINT

We have observed that sometimes the real estate market is a buyers' market and sometimes it is a sellers' market. Furthermore, buyers act differently in a buyers' market than in a sellers' market, and sellers act differently in a sellers' market than in a buyers' market.

At this point, an economist is likely to wonder if what holds true for the real estate market holds true for other markets too. What about the college or university market, or the dating market, or the marriage market? Let's consider each in turn.

THE COLLEGE MARKET

In the college market, students are buyers and the college administration and faculty are sellers. In other words, there is a demand for college education and a supply of college education. Let's suppose that the equilibrium tuition is $1,000 per semester and that the college market is currently in equilibrium. Then, the demand for college education rises. The new equilibrium tuition is, say, $1,200, but the state legislature prohibits colleges or universities under its jurisdiction from raising tuition.

There is now a shortage in the college market. More people will want to attend college than colleges can accommodate. This situation is similar to a sellers' market in real estate where more people want to buy houses than sellers want to sell.

We know what happens when a sellers' market exists in the real estate market, but what might happen in the college market? Are the sellers of a college education likely to demand more than they might otherwise demand from the buyers of a college education? We would expect so.

First, colleges are likely to raise the standards for entering freshmen. Instead of requiring a 3.0 GPA in high school, they may now require a 3.3 GPA.

Second, colleges are more likely to be run the way the administration and faculty want them to be run and less likely to be run the way students want them to be run. How might this difference affect, say, a history course? Suppose a history professor believes her students should write five papers a semester, read four books, take four tests, give two oral presentations, and struggle for hours to complete a very challenging final exam. On the other hand, the professor's students think they should write two papers a semester, read two books, take three tests, give one oral presentation, and work hard, but not struggle, to complete a moderately challenging final exam. The greater the shortage in the college market, the bigger the gap between the equilibrium price in the college market and the tuition paid by the student. The bigger this gap, the more likely the professor will run her course the way she wants to run it. After all, she is in a sellers' market. Any student who doesn't like it can leave. Other students are waiting to fill that spot.

As time passes and the shortage in the college market continues, the professor becomes convinced that she is doing the best for her students by making them work hard to earn a solid college education. (In fact, she may be doing exactly this. Nothing we have said would lead us to believe that she doesn't know what is best for her students.) The professor might even believe that she will never compromise her high teaching standards. She may say, "I teach a solid and challenging course, and I will never lower my standards."

Suppose that at just this time, the demand for a college education begins to fall. It falls so much that colleges are no longer turning away students. As demand falls, equilibrium tuition falls, say from $1,200 per semester to $800 per semester. But again the state legislature keeps tuition fixed at $1,000 per semester. Now we have a buyers' market: colleges have more openings than students who want to occupy those openings. How might this change affect the history professor?

The history professor has seen the enrollment in her class drop from 35 students each semester to only 20 students. She still wants her students to write five papers a semester and so on, and students still want to write only two papers. But now if the professor requires five papers, she cannot be so certain that some students won't simply drop her class. And what will happen then? No students are around to take their places. And without students, are history professors needed? The economist predicts that the history professor will soon lower the standards she said she would never lower.

What changed in our scenario? Did the history professor suddenly see the wisdom of what students were saying all along about research papers, reading books, and tough finals? Or did she simply move from a sellers' market to a buyers' market?

THE DATING MARKET

George Castanza, a major character on the television show *Seinfeld*, was once dating a woman who had a big nose. He told his friend Jerry that he wished the woman would get a nose job.

Well, she did get a get a nose job. In fact, she got two. The first one didn't turn out well; the second one turned out beautifully. When George saw her new, and final, nose, he was amazed at how beautiful she had become and he began to act differently toward her. In particular, George was much more attentive to his girlfriend after she had her new nose than he had been when she had a big nose.

In economic terms, we might say that when his girlfriend had a big nose, George felt that his alternatives for other girlfriends were greater than her alternatives for other boyfriends. Again, let's look at a ratio:

$$X = \frac{\text{George's alternatives}}{\text{Girlfriend's alternatives}}$$

When his girlfriend had a big nose, George was a buyer in a buyers' market. Through his inattentive behavior, he might have been saying, "Hey, it's either me and the way I want to be, or no one."

After his girlfriend got the nose job, though, her alternatives increased. Now George was a buyer in a sellers' market, and he behaved according to his new position.

Is George a shallow man who treats a woman differently depending on whether he or she is in the driver's seat? Well, yes, that's the way George is. But an economist doesn't just drop the topic at this point. An economist asks, "Is everyone a little bit like George? Is George Castanza the epitome of the human race?"

Let's consider how an economist might analyze this situation. If people are like George, then they will behave in predictable ways when they are dating. A person's behavior will be one way with more alternatives than the person he or she is dating and will be a different way with fewer alternatives than the person he or she is dating. With more alternatives, a person is a buyer in a buyers' market and will demand more of and give less to the seller (the person he or she is dating). With fewer alternatives, a person is a buyer in a sellers' market and will demand less of and give more to the seller (the person he or she is dating).

Now let's assume that a person's position in the dating market is a function of only his or her physical beauty. (Yes, beauty is subjective, but most people can agree that Rebecca Romijn-Stamos, as a woman, and Brad Pitt, as a man, are much more attractive than the average woman or man.) The more attractive the person is, the greater market position the person has.

Consider a very attractive woman who dates an unattractive man. In this relationship, the woman has the upper hand. Her alternatives are greater than his alternatives; she is a buyer in a buyers' market. One of two things will happen. Over time, either she will "trade in" the unattractive man for a man she considers a better alternative or she will stay with the man. But if she stays with the man, we predict that she will, on average, demand more and get more from him than he will demand from and get from her.

THE MARRIAGE MARKET

Are persons in a marriage likely to act differently depending on how they evaluate their market positions? Consider the following fictional, but not unrealistic, story.

Two people get married when they are each 21 years old. She goes to work and supports them both while he attends acting school. After he graduates from acting school, he gets a minor role in a movie. The movie is a box-office hit, his performance is superb, and he begins to get offers to do other movies. In time, he becomes a recognizable movie actor. Soon after he has acquired fame and fortune, he asks his wife for a divorce. He says he is in love with and wants to marry someone else. She just happens to be ten years younger than his wife.

What explains this man's behavior? We have left out so many details in the story that it could be almost anything. However, an economist will notice that the story is consistent with one person's market position in a marriage becoming stronger than the other person's. Again, let's consider the alternatives each person in the marriage has at different times. Perhaps when the young couple got married, each at age 21, the number of alternatives for the man and the woman were the same. In essence, neither had a superior market position. In time, though, their situations changed. The man became a well-known movie actor, and his market position strengthened relative to his wife's market position. With his fame and fortune, the man had opportunities that weren't available to him before.

What the Economist Thinks

- *Market behavior exists even outside well-established markets.* For example, "buying" and "selling" behavior can exist in your relationship with a professor, a date, or a spouse.

- *A change in market conditions—say, from a buyers' market to a sellers' market—influences the behavior of both buyers and sellers.* For example, buyers are more likely to demand, and receive, what they want in a buyers' market than in a sellers' market.

- *Thinking in terms of markets (buyers and sellers), market conditions, and market position is helpful to understanding much of what happens in life.*

Questions to Answer

1. Do you think parents behave differently toward their children when the market position of the parents changes? Explain your answer.

2. Consider two countries, *A* and *B*. In country *A*, there is complete separation of church and state and various religions compete for membership. In country *B*, there is one state-recognized religion and all other religions are prohibited. The market position of the state-recognized religion in country *B* is stronger than any one religion in country *A*. What differences, if any, would you predict in the religious climate and practices in country *A* as compared to country *B*? Explain your answer.

3. Many men and women in their thirties, forties, and fifties bemoan the fact that their parents still treat them like little kids. Would their parents be as likely to treat them "like little kids" if grown children could divorce their parents? Explain your answer.

4. "Professors set standards in the classroom that they are not willing to compromise." Do you agree or disagree with the statement? Explain your answer.

5. If you had to summarize succinctly (in one or two sentences) the essence of this chapter, what would you say?

chapter 14

Rational
Men and Women

Economists have a particular view of the world. Specifically, economists assume human beings are rational.

That's right, rational. If you are like most people, when you read the word "rational," you sort of laughed. Most people believe there are enough irrational people out there to make the world kind of nutty at times. Most people—but not economists—equate rational with unemotional, calculating, reasonable, or logical. Irrational, then, becomes the same as emotional, uncalculating, unreasonable, or illogical.

But economists have a different meaning for the word "rational." According to economists, a rational person is one who thinks and acts in terms of costs and benefits. Specifically, a rational person is one who tries to maximize his net benefits in life, or who seeks to maximize his utility or satisfaction.

Again, noneconomists tend to laugh. Do economists mean that human beings go around quickly calculating the costs and benefits of various activities and choose to only undertake activities where the benefits outweigh the costs? Well, yes, this is exactly what economists mean.

Instead of using argument to try to convince people that human beings are rational, economists have chosen a somewhat indirect approach to the subject. They build models to explain real-world events. Economists base their models on the assumption that people are rational; and then the economists have the rational people in their models act, choose, and think about real-world events. In other words, economists people the world of their models with rational individuals.

Now the models that economists build make predictions. If the predictions are validated by real-world data, economists then say: "See, we built a model and in that model we assumed people are rational—that they act and think in terms of costs and benefits and seek to maximize their net benefits. Our model then made certain predictions. We have collected relevant data, and the data validate the predictions. So, we conclude that if the predictions of a model based on rational individuals turn out to be true, then individuals must be rational."

To illustrate the process, we'll build a model based on a rational criminal. This rational criminal, we hold, thinks and acts in terms of costs and benefits. Furthermore, we hold that this criminal has two equations in his head. The first equation relates to the benefits of committing a criminal act, and the second equation relates to the costs of committing a criminal act. We assume the criminal act is burglary. The first equation, the benefit equation, is:

$$EB = Ps \times Loot$$

where *EB* is the expected benefits of burglary, *Ps* is the probability of successfully burglarizing a house (getting into and out of a house with the goods), and *Loot* is the dollar take.

The cost equation looks like this:

$$EC = [Pp \times (I + F)] + AC$$

where *EC* is the expected costs of burglary, *Pp* is the probability of imprisonment, *I* is the income the criminal gives up if caught and imprisoned, *F* is the dollar value the criminal puts on freedom (how much the person would pay to stay out of prison), and *AC* is the anguish cost of committing a burglary.

An economist would say that a criminal simply substitutes various numbers into the equations and then determines whether or not the expected benefits of the criminal act are greater than, less than, or equal to the expected costs. If the expected benefits are greater than the expected costs, the person commits the crime. If the expected benefits are less than the expected costs, the person does not commit the crime. And if the expected benefits equal the expected costs, the person flips a coin: Heads, commit the crime; tails, don't commit the crime.

Let's make up some numbers. Suppose the person sets the following numbers:

$$Ps = 80 \text{ percent}$$
$$Loot = \$400,000$$
$$Pp = 30 \text{ percent}$$
$$I = \$80,000$$
$$F = \$42,000$$
$$AC = \$3,000$$

When we substitute these numbers for the variables in our two equations, we find that the expected benefits (*EB*) equal $320,000 and the expected costs (*EC*) equal $39,600. With these numbers, the person goes ahead and commits the crime.

Now our simple two-equation model of a rational criminal makes some interesting predictions. The model predicts that:

1. If people put more locks on their doors and install more security devices in their homes, the probability of success (Ps) will fall, lowering the benefits of burglary. And, lowering the benefits of burglary will lead to fewer burglaries.

2. If more police are on the streets, the probability of being arrested after committing a crime will rise, and the probability of being imprisoned (Pp) will rise too. Thus, the costs of committing a burglary will rise, and fewer burglaries will be committed.

3. During a recession, incomes usually fall and unemployment usually rises. Thus, the income one forfeits is usually lower during a recession than during boom times. Lower income foregone (I) lowers the cost of burglary, and thus will lead to more burglaries.

4. If prison became more severe (hard labor), a person would pay more to stay out of prison (F). Paying more to stay out of prison raises the cost of burglary, and fewer burglaries will be committed.

More predictions are possible, but you get the point. Just by raising or lowering the values of the different variables in the two equations, we can make predictions that are logically consistent with the model.

Now if we collect relevant data and find that all our predictions are true, we'd have to say that our model has some merit. And what kind of person does the model assume? A rational person.

Models constructed assuming that people are rational might predict accurately or might not. If they predict accurately, it is likely they do so because what they assume about people is correct. A rational choice model of crime that predicts accurately tells us something we might not have been willing to accept earlier: criminals—no matter how irrational, emotional, or unreasonable they seem to us—are rational individuals.

What the Economist Thinks

- *Arguing about whether men and women are rational is useless because so many people misunderstand what it means to be rational.* Instead, it is better to build a model based on rational men and women, make predictions based on the model, and then see whether or not the model predicts correctly.

- *If the model based on rational men and women predicts correctly (especially if it consistently predicts correctly), then—and only then— can we reasonably believe that men and women are rational.*

Questions to Answer

1. Some people say that love is not a rational activity. In other words people "in love" do not think in terms of costs and benefits. Do you agree or disagree? Explain your answer.

2. Smith smokes cigarettes and Jones does not, so obviously both persons cannot be rational. Comment.

3. Can a person be unhappy and rational too? Why or why not?

4. Some people are said to have a bad temper—they "fly off the handle easily" or get unusually angry over little things. Are people who have bad tempers irrational while people who do not have bad tempers rational?

5. Can a person be rational and uninformed? Why or why not?

chapter 15

Rationing Devices

Biology would not exist if living things did not exist. Physics would not exist if motion and matter did not exist. And economics would not exist if scarcity did not exist.

Scarcity is the condition of peoples' wants outstripping the resources available to satisfy those wants. People want goods—things that give them utility—but unfortunately, goods do not fall from the sky. All goods, whether houses, cars, clothes, books, peace on earth, love, or friendships, are produced with resources; and resources are finite. Infinite wants pushing against finite resources—that's scarcity.

How do we decide who gets the available resources in a world where everyone will want these resources in unlimited quantities? Obviously, we need some way to ration the resources. One rationing device is money price. People who are able and willing to pay the money price for the resources will get the resources, and then they will use the resources to produce the goods they want.

If money price did not exist as a rationing device, some rationing device would still be needed because scarcity is always with us. If not money price, then what? Would brute force be a good substitute for money price? Would appearance or race?

Suppose five boys all ask the same high school girl to a dance. How will she decide with whom to go to the dance? She will have to use some rationing device. What will it be?

Suppose 70 boys try out for the boys' baseball team in high school, but only 15 boys can make the team. How does the coach of the team ration the available spots? What rationing device does he use?

Suppose ten thousand students apply to attend Stanford University, but Stanford will only admit some fraction of the number of applicants. What rationing device does it use?

MANY ARGUMENTS IN LIFE ARE ABOUT RATIONING DEVICES

No matter what rationing device is used in any given setting, someone will always argue that some other rationing device should have been used. The boy who doesn't get to go to the dance with the girl will think she put too much emphasis on "looks" and not enough on "personality"—which he believes he has in abundance. The boy who doesn't get on the baseball team will think the coach put too much emphasis on parent donations to the school team and not enough on how fast one can run or how far one can hit a ball. The young woman who doesn't get into Stanford might think that the Admissions Office at the university put too much emphasis on extracurricular activities in high school and not enough on SAT scores.

"THAT'S NOT FAIR."

When something does or doesn't happen to you, to a friend, or to an acquaintance, you often hear someone say, "That's not fair."

Miss Virginia wins the Miss America contest because she's a better singer (in your mind) than Miss North Dakota is, but Miss North Dakota is a better speaker than Miss Virginia. You think Miss North Dakota should have won and that too much emphasis was placed on the talent part of the contest. "That's not fair," you say.

Poor people, we know, cannot buy as many goods and services as rich people can in a world where money price is the rationing device. "That's not fair."

Jimmy studies seven hours for his biology test and gets a C, whereas Karen studies only one hour for the same test and gets an A. "That's not fair."

People say, "That's not fair" in these types of situations because they are upset with the rationing device used to decide who gets what.

NO MATTER WHAT THE RATIONING DEVICE, PEOPLE WILL COMPETE FOR IT

Wherever scarcity exists, a rationing device will be present. And whatever that rationing device turns out to be, people will compete for it.

If money price is the rationing device, then people will compete for money. For example, think of the ways you might compete for money. Perhaps you have decided to go to college because you know that college graduates, on average, earn more than high school graduates. In other words, you have decided to go to college so that you can earn a higher income. And why do you want that higher income? You want a higher income partly because you know that money price is commonly used as a rationing device in the world in which you live.

Suppose that tomorrow, money price were no longer used as a rationing device. Would you have as strong a reason to go to college? Suppose that tomorrow, resources were rationed according to how much weight one could lift. Wouldn't you be likely to drop out of college and enroll in a gym? Wouldn't you be likely to stop studying economics, biology, and sociology and start pumping iron instead?

THE BEAUTY OF MONEY PRICE AS A RATIONING DEVICE

Let's consider two worlds, *A* and *B*. In world *A*, goods are rationed according to need. If someone needs food, he is given food. If someone needs medical attention, she is given medical attention. In world *B*, goods are rationed according to money price. If someone is able and willing to pay the money price for food, he gets the food. If he is either unwilling or unable to pay the money price for food, he does not get the food.

In which world would you rather live?

Many people say that they would prefer to live in world *A*. They say, "World *A* is a more humane and kindly world. In world *B*, only those with money will survive."

But let's think about this for a minute. Is world *A* as humane and kindly as it appears? First, rationing goods according to need raises the question of who or what will decide what constitutes need. Will a political party representative decide what need means? Will only people with an IQ above 150 decide? Mary says she needs a computer. Does her saying it make it so? Do people get computers just because they claim to need them? In a world where need is the rationing device, many wars would be fought to decide who was going to be the person or group to determine need.

Second, if need is the rationing device, why would anyone produce anything? It is easy to see why a person would produce a house in a world where money price is the rationing device. John produces a house in order to sell it for money so that he can use the money to get what he wants. But would John produce a house just to satisfy someone's need for a house? Not likely. Would John be willing to work for weeks to produce a house that is taken from him to satisfy someone's need for a house? Isn't John likely to say, and doesn't he have a right to say, "What's in it for me?"

Third, in a world where need is the rationing device, many people are likely to claim that they are needy. In short, if neediness is the only requirement to get what you want, then no one is going to do anything in life except claim to be needy.

So, how humane and kindly is world *A*? Wars would be fought to decide who was to determine need, no one would produce anything, and everyone would claim to be needy.

Contrast world *A* with world *B*. In world *B*, money price is the rationing device. In this world, many things are likely to be produced because producers will always be happy to get the money that their products fetch.

Houses and cars get built, food gets grown, and people go to medical school to learn how to perform heart surgery for various reasons. But one important reason is because their products or services can be sold for money. Tell the physician that she can't sell her services for money, and see if she comes into the operating room tomorrow. Tell the contractor that he can't sell his houses for money, and see how quickly he shuts down the construction site.

True, poor people can't buy as many goods and services as rich people can buy when money price is used as a rationing device. However, if money price is not used as a rationing device, not many goods will be available for anyone to buy. As odd as it may sound, being poor in a world where money price is the rationing device is probably much better than being poor in a world where need is the rationing device.

What the Economist Thinks

- *A rationing device will always be needed because we live in a world characterized by scarcity.*
- *No matter what the rationing device is, people will compete for it.* Scarcity, rationing devices, and competition all go together.
- *Many arguments in life are fundamentally disagreements about what rationing device should be used.*

Questions to Answer

1. "The disagreement between capitalists and socialists is really no more than a disagreement about rationing devices." Do you agree or disagree with this statement? Explain your answer.

2. Do you think grades in school are rationed? If so, what rationing device is used?

3. "Some rationing devices provide more incentive to people to produce than do other rationing devices." Do you agree or disagree with this statement? Explain your answer.

4. Harvard University uses some combination of money and grades to ration openings in its freshman class. In other words, a person needs certain grades and a certain amount of money in order to be admitted to Harvard. Why doesn't Harvard simply use money as the rationing device?

5. Five people ask you out to dinner for the same night. What rationing device would you use to decide with whom you go to dinner? Is your rationing device "fair"? Why or why not?

chapter 16

Where's Waldo?
Where's the Economics?

Where's Waldo? is the title of a set of children's books. Each page of these books is filled with a scene that includes seemingly hundreds of tiny drawings. A city scene has buses, clothing shops, coffee shops, movie theaters, people walking to and fro, a man selling hot dogs on the corner, a mail carrier delivering mail, and so on and so on. On each page, somewhere in the mass of buses, shops, theaters, and people is Waldo. The objective is to find Waldo.

An economist is much like a child looking for Waldo, except that an economist's book is the real world and she is hunting for economics. She searches for the economics hidden in the myriad scenes of everyday living. Instead of asking, "Where's Waldo?" she asks, "Where's the economics?"

To illustrate, let's take a trip with an economist. Our economist arrives in a cab at the airport for a trip on Delta flight 84, nonstop from Los Angeles to New York.

As he stands at the counter buying his ticket, the economist doesn't see a Delta employee; he sees scarcity. Because scarcity exists, so must a rationing device. One rationing device is dollar price. The economist knows that first-class tickets are priced higher than coach tickets. "Where's the economics?" he asks himself.

The economics relates to supply and demand. There is a supply of and demand for first-class tickets and an equilibrium price too. The same holds for coach tickets. The equilibrium price for first-class tickets is higher than the equilibrium price for coach tickets because demand and supply intersect higher up the graph in the first-class market than they do in the coach market.

AISLE, WINDOW, AND MIDDLE-OF-THE-ROW SEATS

Our economist notices that people handing their tickets to the employee behind the counter ask for either an aisle seat or a window seat, never for a seat in the middle of a row (between the aisle seat and the window seat). Where's the economics?

The economist realizes that the people asking for an aisle seat or a window seat seem slightly apprehensive. They don't ask for these seats the same way they would ask for popcorn in a movie theater. People are sure that if they ask for popcorn in a movie theater, in a few seconds the popcorn will be in their hands. But such assurance does not hold for aisle and window seats. To ask is not necessarily to receive: all the aisle seats and window seats could be taken already. This tells the economist that aisle seats and window seats are rationed not only by dollar price but also by a nonprice rationing device. In this case, the nonprice rationing device is first-come-first-served.

The economist knows that nonprice rationing devices occur when dollar price is not being fully utilized to ration the good, which is another way of saying that dollar price must not be at its equilibrium level. In other words, the price the airline is charging for aisle and window seats might be below equilibrium, thus generating a shortage of aisle and window seats.

Quickly the economist imagines three diagrams in his head. The first is of the middle seat market on the plane. The supply curve is vertical, and the demand curve is downward-sloping. The second diagram is of the aisle seat market on the plane, and the third is of the window seat market on the plane. Are the demand and supply conditions in all three diagrams the same? Not likely. The vertical supply curve in each market diagram might be positioned at the same place, but the demand curve is not. Certainly, the demand for middle seats is lower (closer to the origin) than the demand for either aisle seats or window seats. So if the supply curve in each diagram is positioned the same but the demand curve in the middle seat market is closer to the origin than in either the aisle or window seat market, the equilibrium price in all three markets is not the same. The equilibrium price in the middle seat market is lower.

Now suppose that the airline charges the lower middle-seat equilibrium price in all three markets. For example, suppose $300 is the equilibrium price in the middle seat market and $330 is the equilibrium price in both the aisle and window seat markets. But the airline charges $300 in all three markets. Obviously, the $300 price will be a below-equilibrium price in both the aisle and window seat markets, generating a shortage in each of these markets. In other words, quantity demanded for these seats will be greater than quantity supplied. How will, say, one of the 40 passengers who wants an aisle seat get one of the 35 available aisle seats? She will pay the $300 price and hope that she is one of the first 35 passengers to ask for an aisle seat.

The apprehension the economist notices in the voice of a passenger who asks for an aisle seat is due to a below-equilibrium price that has generated a shortage. Does the passenger know that a too-low price can affect the quality of her speech? Maybe not, but the economist knows.

OVERHEAD COMPARTMENTS

The economist is now in his seat (an aisle seat) watching as other passengers get on the plane. He notices that many carry garment bags. Some passengers with garment bags lay their bags neatly in the overhead compartments; others simply double over their bags and stuff them in the compartments. Why the difference? Are some people slobs and others neat? Is there economics here?

The economist tells himself that obviously some people are less worried about wrinkled clothes than others are. He realizes that people are less worried about wrinkled clothes the lower the opportunity cost of wrinkles. People who are leaving home for, say, a business conference in another city would be more interested in being wrinkle free than people who are returning home from a business conference. The cost of wrinkled clothing is different depending on whether a person is leaving home or returning home. The people who lay out their garment bags carefully are leaving home; the people who double over their garment bags and stuff them haphazardly into the overhead compartment are returning home.

The economist has seen the person who sits next to him stuff his garment bag into the overhead compartment seconds before. He says to the man, "Going home?" The man asks, "How did you know?" The economist skirts the truth and simply says, "Just a guess."

WILL MORE OVERHEAD COMPARTMENT SPACE DO THE TRICK?

The economist overhears another passenger say, "There just isn't enough space in those overhead compartments. The airlines should add more."

Will more space solve the problem of "too little space" in overhead compartments? It would seem to. After all, if too little space is the problem, then won't more space solve the problem?

The economist has a different way of thinking about such things. He knows that if the supply of some good increases, its price will come down. At the new equilibrium, as was the case at the old equilibrium, the quantity supplied of the good will equal the quantity demanded of the good.

For example, suppose apples are the good. There is a demand for and supply of apples. Suppose that the equilibrium price is $1 an apple and that the quantity supplied and the quantity demanded equal 100 apples for each. Now raise the supply of apples. The price falls to 50 cents an apple, and at the new equilibrium, quantity demanded and quantity supplied equal 200 apples for each.

The economist knows that what holds for apples holds for overhead compartment space. At present, a certain "equilibrium price" of overhead compartment space exists and passengers bring enough luggage to fill the entire space. If the supply of space increases, then the price of bringing luggage onto the plane will fall and people will bring more luggage to fit into the added space. So, even with additional space, overhead compartments are likely to be as cramped as they were before the space was added.

GOING TO THE RESTROOM

During his flight, the economist notices that sometimes people are waiting in line to use the restroom but no line exists at other times. What explains what he sees? The obvious answer is that passengers are all served beverages on the plane at about the same time and, therefore, need to use the restroom an hour or so later. There is a problem with this answer, though: people do not have to relieve themselves the second or minute they feel the urge or even an hour after they first feel the urge. Using the restroom is an activity that can be delayed. Can there be an economic explanation?

The economist thinks again of opportunity cost. The lower the opportunity cost of doing something, the more likely that thing will be done; the higher the opportunity cost of doing something, the less likely that thing will be done. The opportunity cost of going to the restroom on an airplane is not constant. It is higher at some times and lower at other times. For example, when a food or beverage cart is in the aisle, the cost of going to the restroom is higher than when a cart is not in the aisle. Passengers will be much more likely to go to the restroom when a food or beverage cart is not in the aisle than when it is. While physiology might have a role in when a person heads for the restroom, the economist knows that cost is important too.

THE CURTAIN

The economist next notices that sometimes the curtain is pulled closed between the first-class section and the coach section of the airplane and it is not closed at other times. Why the difference?

The curtain is pulled closed when food is being served. The person sitting in coach knows that the food service is better in first class than in coach and that first-class passengers have paid for the better service.

Still, a coach passenger might feel uncomfortable seeing a first-class passenger receive wine and steak while she gets a soft drink, a sandwich, chips, and jello.

Seeing others treated better than she is treated—even when they have paid for the better service—may make her trip less enjoyable than it otherwise could be. Anything—no matter how small—that makes the trip less enjoyable may negatively affect the passenger's demand for travel. Leftward-shifting demand curves are not good for airline business. Leftward-shifting demand curves result in lower prices and fewer seats sold—not a good combination for an airline seeking to sell what it produces. Why not simply pull the curtain closed and make it impossible for the sandwich eater to view the steak eater?

AIRLINE MAGAZINES

While browsing through the airline magazines, the economist notices a number of ads for hotels and restaurants. Obviously, hotels and restaurants advertise in airline magazines because people flying in planes are often away from home and in need of a place to sleep and eat.

But, what explains the common theme of the hotel and restaurant ads? Why do restaurants claim to be the "best" restaurant in Dallas, New York, Los Angeles, or wherever? Why do hotels claim to be the "best" hotels? Why the "best"? The economist knows these ads use the word "best" because of a much misunderstood economic concept—price elasticity of demand. Price elasticity of demand is related to the number of substitutes for a good. The fewer substitutes a good has, the lower the price elasticity of demand for that good.

To claim that a restaurant or hotel is the best is to claim that there are no substitutes for it. After all, *best* signifies *one*. There can only be one best, not two, three, or seven. But why would a restaurant or hotel owner want customers to think there were few substitutes? Well, the fewer substitutes the customer thinks there are, the lower the price elasticity of demand for that restaurant or hotel. If the restaurant or hotel owner can get the price elasticity of demand to fall below 1, then certain good things follow.

When price elasticity of demand is less than 1, a seller can raise price and watch total revenue increase. (It is, of course, different when price elasticity of demand is greater than 1. Then, a higher price brings lower total revenue.)

But, of course, total revenue is not really what the seller cares about. He or she cares about profit, which is the difference between total revenue and total cost. What will happen to total cost? It will decline.

Because fewer units of a good are sold at higher prices than at lower prices, it will not be necessary to produce as many units of a good and so total costs decline. In the end, total revenue rises, total costs fall, and profit (the difference between the two) grows.

Thus, while the noneconomist reads that Hotel *X* is the best hotel in Topeka, the economist reads the same words and thinks (1) substitutes, (2) price elasticity of demand, (3) higher prices, (4) higher total revenue, (5) lower total cost, and (6) higher profit. He has found his Waldo.

What the Economist Thinks

- *Economics is everywhere around us; the trick is to find it.*
- *Finding economics can be a lot of fun and is a game worth playing.*

Questions to Answer

1. You buy things from the local grocery store and from the college you attend. Specifically, you buy bread, milk, and soda from the grocery store and educational services from the college. You have to pay both the grocery store and the college for the goods and services you buy. One difference though is that the grocery store sells you the goods you want without asking you what your GPA was in high school or what score you received on the SAT. Colleges do request such information. Where's the economics?

2. An airline often overbooks, that is, it sells 110 tickets for a plane that will only seat 100 people. If 110 people show up for the flight, the airline will try to "buy back" 10 of the 110 tickets. It will offer one price (which can be in dollars for another trip at a later time or an upgraded seat on the next flight) and see how many ticket holders are ready to sell their tickets at that price. If 10 ticket holders are unwilling to sell their tickets at the stated price the airline offers, then the airline will offer a higher price. Where's the economics?

3. Jim regularly loses his temper with Jane but not with Bill, although Jane is not really any more irritating to Jim than Bill is. Where's the economics?

4. People often act differently in big crowds than they do in small groups. Where's the economics?

5. "To be or not to be." Where's the economics?

chapter 17

Drug Bust and SUVs, or the Importance of Thinking in Threes

Almost every economics student learns the law of demand the first or second day of class. The law of demand states that as the price of a good falls, people buy more of the good, *ceteris paribus*. And as the price of a good rises, people buy less of the good, *ceteris paribus*. Nothing hard about the law of demand.

Economics students also learn about what economists call **total revenue**: the number of units sold of a good multiplied times the price of the good. If Jack sells 100 apples at $1 an apple, then Jack's total revenue is $100. Nothing hard about total revenue either.

What happens when the law of demand is considered along with total revenue? Then, economics can show people that what they think is true about drug busts and SUVs might not be true.

DRUG BUSTS AND CRIME

When people talk about illegal drugs and drug busts, they often say that drug users commit crimes to get money to buy illegal drugs. For example, a drug user might burglarize a house in order to get money to buy cocaine. These people then go on to say that if "society" rids itself of drugs, there will necessarily be less crime. After all, no one is going to burglarize a house to get money to buy cocaine if there is no cocaine to buy. In short, reduce the amount of cocaine to buy, and you will cut down on drug-related crimes.

Well, maybe. If there is less cocaine to buy, say, as the result of a successful drug bust, the price of cocaine will rise. (As the supply of any good—bread, milk, or cocaine—falls, the price of the good rises.) However, whether more, less, or the same amount of money is spent on cocaine depends on the price elasticity of demand for cocaine. The price elasticity of demand for a good—cocaine is a good—is the percentage change in the quantity demanded of the good measured against the percentage change in the price of the good.

For example, let's suppose the price of cocaine before the successful drug bust is $50 per unit and 1,000 units are bought and sold each day at this price. So, daily cocaine revenue is $50,000. Now suppose 10 percent of every dollar spent on cocaine is acquired through the commission of some crime. Then, if $50,000 is spent on cocaine each day, one-tenth of this amount, or $5,000, is acquired through criminal activity.

Suppose the drug bust reduces the supply of cocaine for sale to only 600 units of cocaine bought and sold each day. Consequently, the price of cocaine rises to $100 per unit. Now daily cocaine revenue is $60,000. One-tenth of this amount, or $6,000, is acquired through criminal activity.

Did the drug bust reduce drug-related crime? Actually, it did the opposite. More criminal activity is necessary to acquire $6,000 than to acquire $5,000.

We got this outcome because the percentage *decline* in the quantity of cocaine bought and sold (1,000 units to 600 units is a 40 percent decline) is smaller than the percentage *rise* in price ($50 to $100 is a 100 percent rise).

Might the outcome have been different? Could the percentage decline in the quantity of cocaine bought and sold have been larger than the percentage rise in price? Sure, the quantity bought and sold could have fallen from 1,000 units to 100 units (a 90 percent decline) while price increased from $50 to $60 (a 20 percent rise). With these changes, the daily cocaine revenue would have fallen from $50,000 to $6,000, and one-tenth of $6,000 is $600. In this case, crime would have fallen because less criminal activity is needed to acquire $600 than to acquire $5,000.

Finally, as you have perhaps realized, if the percentage fall in the quantity of cocaine bought and sold had been equal to the percentage change in price, there would have been no change in daily cocaine revenue and, therefore, no change in the amount of criminal activity.

So, does a successful drug bust actually reduce drug-related crime? Well, it might, but then again, it might not. A successful drug bust could increase the amount of crime, reduce it, or leave it unchanged. In other words, there are *three* possibilities. The outcome depends on the percentage rise in price and the percentage fall in quantity purchased.

SUVs AND TERRORISM

At the beginning of 2003, some people argued that persons who drive SUVs, or sports utility vehicles, were indirectly aiding terrorists. Their argument was as follows:

1. SUVs usually get low gas mileage.

2. Because SUVs get low gas mileage, their owners have to buy more gasoline (say to get from point X to point Y) than people who drive, say, Honda Civics or Toyota Camrys.

3. Gasoline is a byproduct of oil, and many Middle Eastern countries sell oil.

4. Some of the Middle Eastern countries that sell oil might use part of their oil revenue to finance terrorists that want to harm the United States.

5. SUV drivers are indirectly financing terrorism.

The people who made this argument then proposed that SUV owners should trade in their SUVs for more fuel-efficient cars or that government should force SUV manufacturers to produce more fuel-efficient vehicles.

Now although we might refute this argument that gas-guzzling SUVs indirectly finance terrorism, let's not. Instead, let's just accept it as true. So, if people move from gas-guzzling SUVs to fuel-efficient cars, will they take a bite out of terrorism? Maybe, maybe not.

Let's use some actual amounts to analyze the SUV-terrorism argument. Suppose an SUV gets 13 miles to a gallon of gasoline and the price of a gallon of gasoline is $2. Thus, if an SUV owner wants to drive, say, 130 miles, she must buy 10 gallons of gasoline and pay $20. Compare the SUV to a Civic that gets 26 miles to a gallon. The Civic owner who wants to drive 130 miles only has to buy 5 gallons of gasoline and pay $10. Obviously, the SUV owner turns over more money to terrorists than does the Civic owner.

But haven't we overlooked something? What about the economic concepts of the law of demand and total revenue? Driving is cheaper for the owner of a 26-mpg Civic than it is for the owner of a 13-mpg SUV. Specifically, for the SUV owner, 13 mpg and $2 per gallon for gasoline means every mile driven costs 15.38 cents. In contrast, for the Civic owner, 26 mpg and $2 per gallon for gasoline means every mile driven costs 7.69 cents. If the law of demand holds for driving— and there is evidence that it does—we can then expect Civic owners to drive more miles (say, per week) than SUV owners do. The question is: How many more miles?

Suppose the average SUV owner drives 300 miles per week and the average Civic owner drives 700 miles per week. At $2 a gallon for gasoline, the SUV owner buys 23 gallons of gas a week and pays $46 and the Civic owner buys 27 gallons of gas a week and pays $54.

Obviously, if the SUV owner gives up her SUV, buys a Civic, and becomes the average Civic driver, she will start spending $54 a week on gasoline instead of $46 a week. And isn't that more money in the hands of the terrorists?

The economist simply points out that when the price of driving falls (which it does when drivers move from SUVs to Civics), drivers will drive more. The economist asks, "How much more?" and considers the possible alternatives. If they drive much more, then they may end up spending more, not less, money on gasoline, even though their cars get better gas mileage. If they drive only slightly more, then they will probably spend less money on gasoline. And, of course, the possibility exists that they will not spend any more or any less money on gasoline.

As for drugs busts and crime, there are *three* possibilities for SUVs and terrorism. It is the economist's job to identify and explain these possibilities.

So, were the people who argued that trading in SUVs for Civics would take a bite out of terrorism right? They could be right, but they could be wrong too.

What the Economist Thinks

- *As the price of a good rises, people buy less of the good, and as the price of a good falls, people buy more of the good.* People buy less cocaine at a high price than at a low price; people buy "less driving in their cars" when the price of driving is high than when the price of driving is low.

- *How much money is spent on a good is a function of the price of the good and the number of units bought of the good.*

- *When the price of a good rises, people will buy less of the good, but it is not clear that they will spend less money on the good.* If the price rises by a greater percentage than the quantity purchased falls, they will spend more money on the good. If the price rises by a smaller percentage than the quantity purchased falls, they will spend less money on the good. If the price rises by the same percentage as the quantity purchased falls, they will spend no more and no less money on the good. Many laypersons mistakenly think that when the price of a good rises, people will not only buy less of the good but also spend less money on the good.

Questions to Answer

1. At this moment, renters of apartments in Los Angeles spend a certain dollar amount on rent each month. Let's say this amount is $500 million. Now suppose a major earthquake hits Los Angeles and one-third of all the apartments in the city are destroyed. In other words, for every

100 apartment buildings that existed before the earthquake, now 67 are left standing. As a result, will the total dollar amount spent on rent of apartments in Los Angeles be less than it was before the earthquake? Explain your answer.

2. Suppose a seller can sell either 100 units or 80 units of a good. Is it always better to sell 100 units than 80 units? Explain your answer.

3. Jack says, "If the companies that manufacture and sell gasoline raise the price of gasoline (at the pump), we're just going to have to pay it." Is Jack right? Explain your answer. Do you think Jack is assuming that people buy the same amount of gasoline at higher prices as they do at lower prices?

4. "If the government places a bigger tax on cigarettes, that's not going to get people to stop smoking much." The person who makes this statement seems to believe that the government's objective is to get people to stop smoking. Might the government's objective be to raise tax revenue? And if it is, then wouldn't it be better to tax a good that people would only consume *slightly less* of than to tax a good that people would consume *much less* of? Why or why not?

5. Carla says, "If the minimum wage is raised, fewer people will be hired to work at the minimum wage but employment will not drop off much." Bill says, "If the minimum wage is raised, fewer people will be hired to work at the minimum wage and employment will drop off a lot." Do both Carla and Bill believe that the law of demand holds here? Do both Carla and Bill believe that the percentage change in the minimum wage will be greater than the percentage change in the number of persons working at the minimum wage? Explain your answers.

chapter 18

Is It the Same Everywhere?
Is It the Same All the Time?

Most people know how the game of baseball is played. Basically, the pitcher on one team throws a baseball to a batter on the other team. If the batter hits the ball, he tries to run around all the bases before being tagged out. Of the two teams that play a baseball game at any given time, the team that rounds all the bases more often wins the game.

Now suppose you decide to play a trick on a friend who has never seen a baseball game and has no idea how the game is played. You take him to the baseball field. Unbeknownst to your friend, you have arranged for the two teams to play the game of baseball in a way they have never played it before. Instead of trying to tag out a runner, defensive players will try to hit the runner in the head with the ball. So, when a batter hits the ball and runs to first base, your friend will see the person on the opposing team try to hit the runner in the head with the ball.

Can you imagine what your friend will say about the game of baseball? He'll wonder why anyone would watch such a ridiculous game—much less play it. Your friend will tell you he thinks baseball is a crazy game.

You know that the game your friend thinks is crazy is not really baseball. He only thinks the game is baseball. If he saw a real baseball game, he might like it a lot.

Something similar happens every day in the United States. People criticize something they think is "the market." But what they are really criticizing is a distortion of the market.

NEW YORK APARTMENTS

New York City has a rent stabilization law that functions much like the old rent control law that preceded it. For many of the apartments in New York City, the rent is set at a rate lower than the market equilibrium rate.

Suppose Jack rents one such apartment for $2,000 a month. If he were paying the market equilibrium rent, he would pay $3,500 a month. Jack's been in the apartment for seven years and knows he's getting a good deal.

However, Jack is dissatisfied because the paint on the walls is beginning to peel, the toilet in the guest bathroom doesn't work, and the stairway railing is broken. Jack has reported the problems to his landlord several times, but the landlord hasn't responded to his complaints. So far, the landlord hasn't sent anyone to the apartment to make the necessary repairs.

One night, while out with his friends, Jack mentions the problems he's having with his landlord. He says, "I've called my landlord several times about the repairs that need to be made. Each time, he says he'll have someone come and fix things, but no one ever comes. He's this rich guy who owns the building and is just too cheap to spend a little money to fix up the apartment. I guess it would take away from all the profit he's earning on the building."

After Jack's friends commiserate with him, he goes on to add, "That's the free market for you—nothing but greedy individuals who think only of making a huge profit. The poor renter, consumer, or worker just ends up getting shafted. Why are people so naive to believe that a system based on greed could be any different?"

Jack is criticizing the market because he believes the market is the source of his problems. But what he is criticizing is not really the market. He is unknowingly criticizing the unintended effects of a constraint placed on the market. He is unknowingly criticizing the unintended effects of New York's rent stabilization law.

Let's look at how Jack's situation would have been different if he had been paying the market rent for his apartment. At a market rent of $3,500 a month, the quantity demanded of apartments in New York would equal the quantity supplied of apartments. In this environment, if Jack called his landlord and told him of the problems in the apartment, the landlord would likely have fixed everything quickly. If the landlord didn't make the repairs, Jack could threaten to find another apartment. If Jack moved, the landlord would have to advertise for another renter and would still have to make the repairs before renting to someone else. The landlord would prefer not to incur the extra cost of finding a new tenant. Why incur this cost when the new tenant would be paying the same dollar rent as the old tenant? It would be less costly for the landlord to stay with Jack than to find a new renter.

But the situation is different under the rent stabilization law. Under the law, the landlord of an apartment can raise the rent (above the current rent) before a new tenant takes occupancy. In other words, the landlord might be able to replace Jack's $2,000 a month rent with a new tenant's $2,300 a month rent. Under such conditions, the landlord has a monetary incentive to irritate Jack in the hope of prompting him to find another apartment. Is it any wonder that the landlord is not rushing to fix Jack's apartment?

THE QUESTION THE ECONOMIST ASKS

This book is about how economists think; so, let's consider the thoughts that would go through an economist's mind upon hearing about Jack and his apartment. The first question an economist would ask is: *Is it the same everywhere?* In other words, is Jack's situation in New York City the same as the situations of renters in other cities? Are renters in other cities having the same problems with their landlords that Jack is having with his?

If the situation is *not* the same everywhere—if renters in other cities are not having the same problems that Jack is having in New York City—then the obvious question is: What is different about New York City when compared to other cities? If the economist finds that other cities have *A*, *B*, and *C* and New York City has *A*, *B*, and *D*, well then maybe the variables to focus on to explain Jack's situation in New York City are *C* and *D*. Thus, the economist's question (Is it the same everywhere?) helps her focus on the variable or variables that might explain what she seeks to explain.

In fact, Jack's situation doesn't occur everywhere. Specifically, it doesn't occur (nearly as often, or to the same degree) in cities where renters pay market rents.

GAS PRICES AND ANOTHER QUESTION THE ECONOMIST ASKS

Every time gas prices rise, someone will say, "Oil companies raised the price of gas just so they could make more money. Those oil company executives sit around their big wooden tables in their luxurious company boardrooms dictating higher prices to the little guy who has to buy gas to get to work at seven in the morning. They're all just greedy!"

A variant of the economist's question (Is it the same everywhere?) is relevant here. This question is: *Is it the same all the time?*

In other words, can oil company executives raise the price of gas any time they want? Obviously, the answer is no. If they could, wouldn't they have raised the price last week or last month? After all, if higher gas prices are good for the oil companies, wouldn't they raise prices sooner rather than later? Also, if they could raise the price of gas any time they want, why would the oil companies raise the price only 10 cents? Why not 20 cents, 30 cents, or even $3? If higher prices are always better than lower prices, then why not simply raise the price to $50 a gallon?

The fact that oil company executives cannot raise prices at any time and cannot raise prices by any amount tells the economist they are constrained. But constrained by what? The answer is supply and demand. Higher gas prices are a consequence of higher demand for gasoline or lower supply of gasoline or both. Let's consider these possibilities.

Higher demand must come from consumers, not from oil company executives. If people want to drive their cars more, the demand for gasoline will rise and, assuming that nothing else changes, gas prices will rise.

But, what about supply? If the supply of a good falls, its price will rise. Can't oil company executives reduce the amount of oil they supply to the market? Won't this reduction drive up the price of gasoline at the pump?

Well, sure they can do this, but there are two reasons why they won't. The first reason has to do with the law; the second reason relates to money.

Let's look at the law. Suppose oil company executives get together and decide to reduce the amount of oil they supply to the market. They would be conspiring against the public, or entering into a cartel agreement, which is illegal under antitrust laws. Someone would find out what the oil company executives are doing, and government officials would soon haul everyone off to court and later, prison.

But even if the antitrust laws were struck down tomorrow, oil company executives would still have a difficult, if not impossible, time curtailing the supply of oil flowing to the market. Why? Because of our second reason.

To explain, let's suppose oil company executives get together on Monday and agree to curtail supply. Their thinking is: "We will reduce the amount of oil we supply to the market, and soon the price of oil will rise. Then, we can sell our oil (albeit not as much oil) at a higher price." In other words, instead of selling, say, 20,000 barrels of oil at $25 a barrel, they might sell 15,000 barrels of oil at $40 a barrel. As anyone can calculate, 15,000 barrels of oil times $40 is a larger dollar amount than 20,000 barrels of oil times $25.

Having made this deal on Monday, some oil executives will be scratching their heads on Tuesday. Some will think: "Why not let the other oil companies reduce production while I increase production? Then I can sell more oil at higher prices, which is better than selling less oil at higher prices." After thinking this, the executives will realize that the other oil executives can think the same thing. Because they are afraid their competitors will cheat on the agreement, each oil company executive will want to get the jump on the others and cheat first. And so the agreement made on Monday will be broken on Tuesday.

The truth is that gas prices are determined much the way house prices are determined. For example, in southern California, house prices rose sharply in the late 1990s. Although house prices were rising at an annual rate of between 10 and 25 percent in some cities, people almost never heard anyone say that house sellers were trying to gouge the house-buying public by setting higher house prices. (No one seemed to think that house sellers were mean, nasty, and greedy.) Instead, most people seemed to conclude that higher house prices were the result of the demand for houses rising at a faster rate than the supply of houses. In other words, higher house prices were a market (supply-and-demand) phenomenon.

When you are part of any market, you are either a buyer or a seller. Sometimes the market is on your side: If you are a buyer, prices are falling; if you are a seller, prices are rising. House sellers can have the market on their side today but not tomorrow. The same holds for oil company executives. Today, the demand for oil and gas at the pump rises; tomorrow, it falls. And so, today price rises; tomorrow price falls.

If the price rises because oil company executives are mean, nasty, and greedy, then it must be true that when the price falls, oil company executives changed their spots and became nice, sweet, and altruistic. Although most people might not like this conclusion, it is the logical one. A more accurate statement is that oil company executives are probably always a little greedy but their greediness is irrelevant to the price of gasoline at the pump.

What the Economist Thinks

- *People sometimes unjustly criticize the market because they do not have a clear understanding of what the market is and what it can and cannot do.*

- *To explain things correctly, it is important to ask questions that focus on differences.* Two such questions are: *Is it the same everywhere? Is it the same all the time?*

Questions to Answer

1. In this chapter, we state that sometimes people unjustly criticize the market because they do not understand what the market is and what it can and cannot do. One explanation for why people do not understand the market is that they do not have the ability to understand it. This is probably not the correct explanation because the same people who do not understand the market often understand concepts that are much more complex than the market is. What is the economic explanation for why people who are capable of understanding the market do not understand the market? In other words, if a person has the ability to learn X but does not learn X, then what explains the person not learning X?

2. Someone says, "Shortages are caused by greedy sellers keeping their goods off the market until price rises." What question is an economist likely to ask upon hearing these words? How does the question reduce the chances of the economist incorrectly explaining shortages?

3. Hotel operators raise their room rates during the peak season and lower their room rates during the off-peak season. Are hotel operators greedy during the peak season and altruistic during the off-peak season, or are they likely to be greedy during both seasons? Explain your answer.

4. Gordon Gekko, a character in the movie *Wall Street*, said, "Greed is good." Would an economist agree or disagree with Gekko? Would an economist qualify his answer? Explain your answer.

5. "Asking *Is it the same everywhere?* and *Is it the same all the time?* is a way of focusing on differences." Do you agree or disagree with this statement? Explain your answer.

chapter 19

Gifts, Trades, and Transfers

Scarcity is the condition where peoples' wants are greater than the resources available to satisfy those wants. But, what exactly do people want? The economist's answer is that people want goods. **Goods** are those things that give people utility or satisfaction. Goods can be tangible or intangible. Both a house and love are goods; the house is a tangible good, and love is an intangible good.

According to economists, people can get goods in only three ways. We discuss these ways in this chapter.

GIFTS

People give and get gifts. The gifts are always goods—things the gift giver believes will make the gift recipient better off, happy, or more nearly satisfied. So, one way to get a good is to be a gift recipient. In other words, to have others give you gifts. But to be a gift recipient, you have to be in someone's utility function in a positive way.

To illustrate, let's consider Stephanie, who gains utility from getting more of many things. Stephanie gains utility if she gets more money, more clothes, or more vacation time. Also, Stephanie gains utility if her sister, Alice, becomes better off. In other words, in Stephanie's utility function are (1) money, (2) clothes, (3) vacation time, and (4) Alice, among other things.

Because Alice is in Stephanie's utility function, one way for Stephanie to gain utility is to have Alice gain utility. And one way to have Alice gain utility is to give her a good that she wants. So, for example, if Stephanie gives Alice a gift of clothes, Alice will become happier, and then Stephanie, witnessing Alice's increased happiness, will become happier (gain utility) too.

Everyone is likely to be in someone's utility function in a positive way. A son might be in the utility function of both his mother and his father. A sister might be in her brother's utility function. A father might be in his son's utility function.

The more utility functions you are in, the more gifts you are likely to get. So, it is better to be in the utility functions of 20 people than in those of only 10 people. After all, a chief objective in life is to get as many goods as you can, and the more utility functions you are in, the more goods you will get as gifts. (By the way, if you read the previous sentence and did not recoil, then you are beginning to think like an economist. Many people, upon reading the words "a chief objective in life is to get as many goods as you can," would have wondered what callous, selfish person could have written such a crass statement. But you know that goods are more than just big houses, fancy cars, and diamond rings; you know that love, friendship, and peace on earth are goods too.)

But the sad truth is that most of us are not in a lot of peoples' utility functions. In a world of more than 6 billion people, most of us are in the utility functions of fewer than 10 people. So, most of us must find other ways to get goods, which brings us to trade.

TRADES

One way to get goods is by trading. But before you can trade for a good, you must have something to trade. Usually, people trade one good for another good. Trading is most easily understood by looking at a barter (or moneyless) economy.

Suppose Karen has apples (a good) and wants oranges (another good). She finds someone who has oranges and wants apples, and then trades with this person. How did Karen get the apples she traded for oranges? Either she received the apples as a gift from someone (someone whose utility function she was in) or else she produced the apples. Because few of us get goods as gifts, Karen likely got the apples by producing them. For most people, producing precedes trading.

Economics is about many things, but mainly it is about producing and trading. Every economics textbook is likely to devote many pages to producing and trading.

TRANSFERS

Can people get goods any other way besides receiving them as gifts or trading for them? Yes, people can get goods through effecting (involuntary) transfers of goods from others to themselves. Transfers can be either illegal or legal.

An example of an illegal transfer is theft. Suppose Conrad, a burglar, breaks into your house when you are away and takes your new computer, your television set, and the $200 you had hidden in a sock in a drawer. You were not willing to give these goods to Conrad as a gift. (You don't even know Conrad, and if you did, he certainly wouldn't be in your utility function in a positive way.) You did not enter into any trades with Conrad. Instead, Conrad simply transferred certain goods from you to himself—without asking.

Legal transfers can take different forms. But legal transfers are not necessarily any more voluntary than illegal transfers.

To illustrate, let's consider tariffs, which are simply "taxes" placed on imported goods. Economists have shown diagrammatically and mathematically that tariffs take from domestic consumers and give to domestic producers and to government. Specifically, tariffs reduce the amount of consumers' surplus (or benefits) that domestic consumers receive from trading, increase the amount of producers' surplus (or benefits) that domestic producers receive from trading, and generate revenue for the government. Moreover, the losses to consumers from tariffs are greater than the sum of the benefits to domestic producers and government. For example, consumers might lose, say, $4 billion while producers and government (together) gain $3 billion.

Tariffs are legal transfers. While Conrad may end up in jail if he is caught stealing from your house, neither domestic producers nor government officials will end up in jail because of tariffs.

Legal transfers such as tariffs sometimes distort the free trades that individuals want to make with each other. For example, suppose American consumers want to buy a good from a British producer for, say, $100. The American producer who competes with this British producer convinces the American government to place a tariff on the British producer's good. Instead of paying $100 for the British-produced good, American consumers now have to pay $130. How does the tariff benefit the American producer? Obviously, if American consumers have to pay more for the British producer's good, they will be less willing and able to buy the good. American consumers might then look more favorably on the competitive good produced by the American producer.

Legal transfers can also take the form of direct subsidies. To illustrate, an American farmer would likely prefer to sell his good for $5 a bushel instead of the market price of $4 a bushel. However, American consumers are likely to refuse to pay the additional dollar a bushel. The American farmer might then go to the U.S. Congress and argue that he needs an extra $1 more per bushel to survive. The U.S. Congress could be convinced by the farmer's arguments and agree to pay the farmer $1 more per bushel for his good. Thus, the American taxpayer would be forced to pay what the American consumer had declined to pay.

LOOKING FOR GIFTS, TRADES, AND TRANSFERS

An earlier chapter describes the economist's version of *Where's Waldo?* Instead of looking for Waldo in pictures in books, the economist looks for economics in the real world. Is there economics in the classroom? on an airplane? in a movie theater? Is there economics that relates to gifts, trades, or transfers? Let's consider some possibilities.

In 1991, Saddam Hussein, the ruler of Iraq, started to move Iraqi troops into Kuwait, a neighboring country. Did this move have anything to do with gifts, trades, or transfers? Most probably it had to do with transfers: Saddam Hussein was attempting to transfer some or all of the Kuwaiti oil from the Kuwaitis to himself.

Jack and Jill carpool to work. One week Jack drives, the next week Jill drives. Jack and Jill are trading, although no money changes hands. Jack trades his driving one week for Jill driving the next week.

A company hires seven lobbyists to go to Washington, D.C., to argue its case for government assistance in the development of a new medicine. The company is seeking to effect a transfer.

A mother puts $50 in an envelope, along with a birthday card, and sends it to her daughter who is away at college. Obviously, the mother is giving a gift to her daughter.

What the Economist Thinks

- *There are three ways to get goods: (1) receive a gift, (2) trade one good for another good, (3) effect a transfer of a good from someone else to oneself.*

- *Much of life can be analyzed in terms of gifts, trades, and transfers.*

Questions to Answer

1. If Sam steals $100 from Bob, Sam is engaged in transferring $100 from Bob to himself. We would expect Bob to dislike such a transfer. Can you think of a transfer that Bob wouldn't mind? Or are all transfers necessarily involuntary on the part of the person who has something transferred away from him?

2. Would you prefer to live in country *A*, where 90 percent of all activity is trading, or in country *B*, where 90 percent of all activity is transferring? Explain your answer. Do you think that in some real-world countries the trade-to-transfer ratio is higher than it is in other countries? Explain your answer.

3. How can someone get into a person's utility function in a positive way? Stated differently, assume Susan is in Bill's utility function in a positive way. Does Bill randomly choose who will be in his utility function in a positive way? If not, then how does he "choose"?

4. What does it mean if someone is in a person's utility function in a negative way?

5. Define both "love" and "hate" in terms of the way a person appears in another person's utility function. Explain your definitions.

chapter 20

There Are No $10 Bills on the Sidewalk

Once upon a time, a man rubbed a lamp and out came a genie in a puff of smoke. The genie said, "I will grant you three wishes. However, there is one condition. Whatever you wish for, your ex-wife will get double."

The man was both happy and sad to hear what the genie said. He was happy that he would get whatever he wished for, but he was sad that whatever he wished for, his wife would get double. Still, he proceeded with his first wish, which was for $10 million in cash. The man received his $10 million in cash, and his ex-wife got $20 million in cash.

Months later, the genie went to the man and asked him for his second wish. The man said that he wished for a beautiful palace on the top of a hill. Again, the genie granted the man his wish. But, then, he also bestowed two beautiful palaces, each on top of a hill, to the man's ex-wife.

Months passed before the man made his third wish. "What is your third wish?" the genie asked the man one day. The man thought for a few minutes. Then he perked up and said, "For my third wish, I want you to beat me half to death."

After chuckling, ask yourself: Did the man with the three wishes think like an economist?

The answer, of course, is no. An economist's first wish—not his third—would have been to beat him half to death. The reason is obvious. The ex-wife would not have gotten $20 million in cash and two beautiful palaces had the man's first wish been to beat him half to death.

Assuming the man disliked his ex-wife and wished her dead (which is clear from the joke), he would have been better off (maximized his utility or satisfaction) had he told the genie to beat him half to death before wishing for the money and palaces. In short, by not making his third wish first, the man gave up an opportunity to make himself better off.

An economist would not have overlooked this opportunity. In fact, economists believe that no one overlooks an opportunity to make himself or herself better off.

One way to summarize how economists think in this situation is: Economists believe that there are no $10 bills on the sidewalk. If you doubt that what economists believe is true, then simply ask yourself how many $10 bills you have seen on the sidewalk. Our guess is none. If a $10 bill were on the sidewalk, someone would pick it up so fast that few other people would have a chance to see it. Most people will not pick up litter on the sidewalk, many will not pick up a penny on the sidewalk, and no one will pick up chewed gum on the sidewalk. But everyone who sees a $10 bill on the sidewalk will pick it up. No one will forfeit the opportunity of getting $10 for the cost of leaning down and picking it up.

However, the man with the three wishes did not pick up the $10 bill on the sidewalk. He had the opportunity of getting rid of his ex-wife with his first wish. He could have denied her the money and goods he would soon have as his own. But he chose not to take advantage of his opportunity—that is, wishing for the genie to beat him half to death. He chose not to pick up the $10 bill.

At this point, critics often argue that perhaps the man with the three wishes did not pick up the $10 bill because he did not immediately see it lying there on the sidewalk. In other words, it didn't dawn on him until after he had already made his first two wishes that he could have wished for the genie to beat him half to death *before* wishing for the money and palaces.

Could the critics be right? Well, they could be, but they probably are not. People are strongly motivated—one might say they have a sixth sense—to identify valuable opportunities immediately. After all, they have an incentive to do just that, so they are unlikely to be unaware for many minutes after a valuable opportunity presents itself.

HOW DOES THE $10 BILL PRINCIPLE HELP THE ECONOMIST?

You may be thinking, "Okay, economists believe that there are no $10 bills on the sidewalk. So what good does it do an economist to think this way?" Actually, economists use the $10 bill principle in literally hundreds of analyses.

To illustrate, let's review a topic from Chapter 7. When discussing houses in San Diego and Buffalo, we calculated a util-to-price ratio (util return). Because of climate differences, the util-to-price ratio was higher in San Diego than in Buffalo; that is, people received more utility per dollar in San Diego than in Buffalo. Thus, people would start to move from Buffalo to San Diego because living in San Diego would be a "better deal" than living in Buffalo.

The $10 bill principle was implicit in this discussion. After all, saying the util-to-price ratio is higher in San Diego than in Buffalo is really the same as saying a $10 bill is lying on the sidewalk in San Diego just waiting to be picked up.

THE $10 BILL PRINCIPLE AND THE LAW OF DEMAND

There is probably no more important economic law and no economic law that has greater applications than the law of demand. But the law of demand (which is empirically verified every hour of every day) is really at heart the $10 bill principle.

To illustrate, suppose there are two goods, apples and oranges. Currently, Jones is consuming 10 apples and 10 oranges. Her tenth apple brings her 30 utils, and her tenth orange brings her 30 utils. Currently, the price of an apple is 50 cents and the price of an orange is 50 cents. So, the util-to-price ratio for each good is the same.

Suppose the price of an apple falls to 45 cents. Now, the util-to-price ratio for apples is higher than the util-to-price ratio for oranges. In other words, Jones gets more utils per penny from apples than from oranges.

A "$10 bill" (so to speak) has just presented itself to Jones. She can buy one less orange, thus saving 50 cents, and then use 45 of the 50 cents saved to buy an apple. The 45-cent apple gives Jones as many utils (30) as the 50-cent orange but has an added plus: 5 cents left over that can be used to buy other goods that give her utility.

If Jones picks up the "$10 bill," she is living the law of demand. She is buying more of a good whose price has declined.

Will Jones pick up the $10 bill? As stated earlier, there is plenty of empirical proof behind the law of demand, so the Joneses of the world must be picking up the $10 bills all the time.

THE $10 BILL PRINCIPLE AND CHEATING ON CARTEL AGREEMENTS

Chapter 18 discusses the reason why gas prices rise. The following two paragraphs are from that discussion and explain why a cartel agreement is unlikely to hold.

To explain, let's suppose oil company executives get together on Monday and agree to curtail supply. Their thinking is: "We will reduce the amount of oil we supply to the market, and soon the price of oil will rise. Then, we can sell our oil (albeit not as much oil) at a higher price." In other words, instead of selling, say, 20,000 barrels of oil at $25 a barrel, they might sell 15,000 barrels of oil at $40 a barrel. As anyone can calculate, 15,000 barrels of oil times $40 is a larger dollar amount than 20,000 barrels of oil times $25.

Having made this deal on Monday, some oil executives will be scratching their heads on Tuesday. Some will think: "Why not let the other oil companies reduce production while I increase production? Then I can sell more oil at higher prices, which is better than selling less oil at higher prices." After thinking this, the executives will realize that the other oil executives can think the same thing. Because they are afraid their competitors will cheat on the agreement, each oil company executive will want to get the jump on the others and cheat first. And so the agreement made on Monday will be broken on Tuesday.

Where is the $10 bill in this analysis? Obviously, it is implicit in the words, "As anyone can calculate, 15,000 barrels of oil times $40 is a larger dollar amount than 20,000 barrels of oil times $25."

In fact, in this case, the $10 bill is really the difference between 15,000 times $40 and 20,000 times $25. It is $100,000. If there are no $10 bills on the sidewalk, then how many $100,000 bills are there likely to be?

THE $10 BILL PRINCIPLE AND HIRING

Suppose you own a firm that hires labor. How much labor would you hire? Would you hire 10, 20, 30, or 100 employees?

The noneconomist's answer is you should hire as many employees as you need to produce your good. But this answer isn't likely to help you. First, it doesn't tell you exactly how many employees to hire. Second, although it is difficult to determine how many units of your good you ought to produce, this answer assumes it is obvious.

An economist answers the question more precisely. He says that you should continue to hire employees as long as an additional employee hired brings more money "into" the firm than it costs to hire that additional employee. In other words, if, say, the tenth employee produces output that can be sold for $100 and you need pay her only $40, then, by all means, hire the tenth employee.

In economics, the dollar value of the output that an additional employee produces is called the value of her marginal product. What is paid to the additional employee is her wage. So, as long as the value of an employee's marginal product is greater than her wage, it is worth hiring the employee. Where is the $10 bill principle here? Well, think in terms of dollars: the tenth employee produces output that can be sold for $100 and her wage is $40. In this case, a $60 bill is lying on the sidewalk. Will the owner of a firm, who wants to maximize profit, lean over to pick up $60 lying on the sidewalk? Would you?

Is It Over Yet?

Economists write and tell stories. Not stories about spies in Europe, lovers in the Caribbean, or ghosts in Victorian houses, but stories nonetheless. Economists' stories are about men and women who buy and sell.

Just as every good novelist must know when and how to end a story, so must every economist. When an economist is writing a story about buyers or sellers, how does he know when to end the story? How does he know when the story is over?

An economist simply asks this question: Are there any $10 bills on the sidewalk that haven't been picked up yet? If there are, then the story isn't over. Surely, someone will be along in a matter of seconds and pick up the $10 bill. Only when all the $10 bills have been picked up (which, as we mention earlier, happens so quickly that few of us see any $10 bills lying around) is the story over.

Think back to the story of buying oranges and apples. At first, the util-to-price ratio for each good is the same; then the price falls. Is the story over one second after the price falls? No, a $10 bill is still on the sidewalk. The $10 bill is in the form of the util-to-price ratio being greater for apples than for oranges. Only when the util-to-price ratio for both goods is once again the same will there be no $10 bills on the sidewalk. Only then is the story over.

Think back to the story of hiring employees. The value of the employee's marginal product is greater than her wage. Is the story over yet? No, a $10 bill shows up on the sidewalk in the form of the positive difference between the value of the employee's marginal product and her wage. When the value of the employee's marginal product is equal to her wage, then the $10 bill will be gone and the story will be over.

What the Economist Thinks

- *People do not ignore opportunities to make themselves better off, especially when the benefits of making themselves better off are greater than the costs of making themselves better off.* This idea is captured in the $10 bill principle. The cost of leaning over and picking up a $10 bill lying on a sidewalk is low, and the benefits are (relatively) high. So everyone who sees a $10 bill on the sidewalk will likely pick it up.

- *If everyone will pick up a $10 bill on the sidewalk, then the chances are that less than a second will elapse between when a $10 bill falls to the sidewalk and when it is picked up.* If the time is so short, we ought not observe many $10 bills on the sidewalk—and, of course, we don't.

- *Economists determine when the economic stories they write are over by asking: Is there a $10 bill on the sidewalk?* If the answer is yes, the story is not yet over. (Someone will pick up the $10 bill before you can blink an eye. Identify that person in the story.) If the answer is no, the story is over.

Questions to Answer

1. "If the $10 principle did not hold, then neither would the law of demand." Do you agree or disagree with this statement? Explain your answer.

2. Few people, if any, have literally seen a $10 bill lying on the sidewalk, but many people have seen a penny lying on the sidewalk. Why a penny and not a $10 bill?

3. A newspaper headline reads: "Lottery up to $100 million—people stand in line for hours waiting to buy tickets." What, if anything, does this headline have to do with the $10 bill principle?

4. Economists argue that a firm will produce an additional unit of a good as long as the additional revenue (or marginal revenue) from an additional unit is greater than the additional cost (marginal cost) of producing an additional unit. What does this have to do with the $10 bill principle?

5. While no one will ignore a $10 bill on the sidewalk, some people might see the $10 bill before others see it. For example, a person with 20/20 vision might see it before a person with 40/80 vision. Do you think there is a difference in "vision" (among people) when it comes to other (nonliteral) "$10 bills"? Do successful entrepreneurs "see" better than the rest of us? Explain your answers.

chapter 21

Ratios:
More Than
Twice As Good

Suppose you learn that the federal budget deficit is $300 billion. Your first response might be to say, "Wow, that's a large deficit." But if you compare the budget deficit to, say, gross domestic product (GDP), your reaction might be different. If the budget deficit is $300 billion and GDP is $11 trillion, then the budget deficit seems smaller. The deficit-to-GDP ratio is 0.027.

Or, suppose someone tells you that Jones has a personal debt of $1 million. Upon first hearing this, you might think that Jones is in debt up to his neck. But if Jones's annual income is $10 million, then his personal debt is only one-tenth of his income. Jones's debt is similar to a $5,000 debt for a person with an annual income of $50,000.

Finally, suppose you learn that Smith's annual income has increased from $50,000 to $80,000 in one year. This $30,000, or 60 percent, rise in income might seem substantial. You might think that Smith is definitely better off. But let's compare Smith's rise in income to the general rise in prices. Suppose prices have risen by 80 percent over the year. Does Smith's increase in income look as good now? If Smith's income rises by 60 percent but prices rise by 80 percent, then Smith is actually worse off, not better off.

Economists want to see the whole picture as often as possible. In each example above, looking at a single thing gives only one small picture. But, comparing the single thing to something else gives a different, more complete picture. To acquire a more complete picture, economists often use ratios to compare one thing to something else. Comparisons using ratios put things into context and provide more meaningful information. The following sections discuss six of the economist's favorite ratios.

RATIO OF PERCENTAGE CHANGE IN DOLLAR INCOME TO PERCENTAGE CHANGE IN PRICES

As the example of Smith shows, rising dollar income does not mean as much when prices are rising as when prices are either stable or falling. A more accurate picture of how a person is affected by a rise in dollar income is given by the ratio of percentage change in dollar income to percentage change in prices:

$$\frac{\text{Percentage change in dollar income}}{\text{Percentage change in prices}}$$

If the numerator in the ratio is the same as the denominator (the ratio equals 1), then the person is neither better off nor worse off (in terms of what his or her dollars will buy). If the numerator is less than the denominator (the ratio is less than 1), then the person is worse off (he or she has less buying power). If the numerator is greater than the denominator (the ratio is greater than 1), then the person is better off (he or she has more buying power).

RATIO OF QUANTITY DEMANDED TO QUANTITY SUPPLIED

Economists often talk in terms of the quantity demanded and the quantity supplied of some good or service. Taking the two together, we have a ratio:

$$\frac{\text{Quantity demanded}}{\text{Quantity supplied}}$$

When the numerator is greater than the denominator, there is a shortage in the market. When the numerator is less than the denominator, there is a surplus in the market. And when the numerator equals the denominator, the ratio is 1 and equilibrium exists in the market.

Is thinking in terms of a ratio important when discussing markets? Well, consider how little information is communicated by saying, "Quantity demanded is 100 units." What does this information do for us? Absolutely nothing (say it again). We need to know what quantity supplied is before we know anything about the state of the market.

RATIO OF PRICES IN ONE YEAR TO PRICES IN ANOTHER YEAR

As President of the United States, Abraham Lincoln earned $25,000 a year, John Kennedy earned $100,000 a year, and George W. Bush earns $400,000 a year. George W. Bush is paid better than Lincoln and Kennedy were paid, right? Well, it would seem so if only the dollar incomes of each are compared.

But prices were much lower in 1863 (when Lincoln was President) than in 1960 (when Kennedy was President). And prices in both 1863 and 1960 were lower than in 2002 (one year when Bush was President). If we really want to know which President was paid better, shouldn't we try to adjust for price differences?

The economist thinks so. To find out how much prices have changed over a time period, the economist computes this ratio:

$$\frac{\text{Price index in later year}}{\text{Price index in earlier year}}$$

For example, the price index in 2002 was 179.8; the price index in 1960 was 29.9. Computing our ratio, we get 6.01. This means that prices were 6.01 times higher in 2002 than they were in 1960. A good that cost $6 in 1960 would cost slightly more than $36 in 2002. A $10 meal in 1960 would cost $60 in 2002. Giving a restaurant server a $1 tip in 1960 was equivalent to giving a $6 tip in 2002. And, of course, a President who earned $100,000 in 1960 would be equivalent to a President earning $601,000 in 2002.

But George W. Bush didn't earn $601,000 in 2002; he earned $400,000. So, who was better paid, Kennedy or Bush? Kennedy was better paid. Earning $100,000 in 1960 is the same as earning $601,000 in 2002.

RATIO OF PERCENTAGE CHANGE IN QUANTITY DEMANDED TO PERCENTAGE CHANGE IN PRICE

The price elasticity of demand is discussed in two earlier chapters. The ratio for the price elasticity of demand coefficient is:

$$\frac{\text{Percentage change in quantity demanded}}{\text{Percentage change in price}}$$

If the numerator is greater than the denominator (the ratio is greater than 1), then demand (for a good between two prices) is elastic. If the numerator is less than the denominator (the ratio is less than 1), then demand is inelastic. Finally, if the numerator is equal to the denominator (the ratio is equal to 1), then demand is unit elastic.

Does it matter whether demand is elastic, inelastic, or unit elastic? As an earlier chapter explains, it certainly does matter when considering the effect on total revenue of a change in price. For example, suppose a college is thinking about raising its tuition because, it believes, this will increase its overall tuition revenue. However, if the demand for education at the college is elastic (between the current tuition and the new higher tuition), then the opposite will occur. Tuition revenue will decline.

RATIO OF AVERAGE VARIABLE COST TO PRICE

Suppose a firm's average variable cost is $10 at the quantity of output it is producing and selling. Does this information tell you anything particularly important? Not really. It's sort of like learning that Farmer Jones harvested 5,000 apples today.

However, we obtain useful information by looking at a firm's average variable cost in relation to the price the firm charges for each unit of the good it sells:

$$\frac{\text{Average variable cost } (AVC)}{\text{Price } (P)}$$

If the numerator is greater than the denominator (the ratio is greater than 1) then the firm's total variable cost (AVC multiplied times the quantity of output the firm produces) is greater than the firm's total revenue (price multiplied times quantity of output). Given this situation, the firm is better off shutting down its operation and losing only its fixed costs than continuing to operate and losing not only its fixed costs but also some variable costs.

If the numerator is less than the denominator (the ratio is less than 1), then the firm's total revenue is greater than its total variable cost. With this information, the owner of the firm realizes that the firm is better off if it continues to operate. If the firm shuts down, it will lose all its fixed costs. But if it continues to operate, it will (at minimum) not lose its entire fixed costs because some of the revenue over variable costs can be applied to fixed costs.

In short, the AVC-to-P ratio helps a firm decide whether to shut down its operation or continue to produce and sell its goods. In a way, this ratio performs the same job for a firm that a body thermometer performs for a person. It gives the firm a good idea of how well or how poorly it is doing.

RATIO OF MARGINAL REVENUE TO MARGINAL COST

Suppose you are the owner of a firm that produces telephones. To find out how many phones you should produce, you could compute the marginal revenue-to-marginal cost ratio:

$$\frac{\text{Marginal revenue}}{\text{Marginal cost}}$$

When the numerator is greater than the denominator (the ratio is greater than 1), then a firm should continue to produce and sell additional units of the good. When the numerator is less than the denominator (the ratio is less than 1), then a firm knows that it has produced too many units of a good. It ought to cut back its production until the numerator equals the denominator (the ratio equals 1).

WILL IT LAST?

Some people believe that "what has happened" will continue to happen—seemingly forever. If the price of stock X has risen by 10 percent each month for the past 10 months, some people believe the stock's price will continue to rise for the next 10 months, the next 20 months, or even the next 100 months. The economist, however, puts events into perspective—and into historical context—by looking at the ratio of one thing to another over time.

For example, economists often look at a stock's price in terms of its earnings. In short, they look at a price-earnings (P-E) ratio:

$$\frac{\text{Price per share of stock}}{\text{Earnings per share of stock}}$$

Suppose the P-E ratio for stock X is usually 20; that is, the price of stock X is usually 20 times its earnings. Then, the price of stock X begins a rise that, at last count, has gone on for 10 months. If earnings have not changed during this time, obviously the numerator in the P-E ratio is rising while the denominator is staying constant. The P-E ratio will rise, say, from 20 to 40.

Along comes the person who tells you that you ought to buy stock X right away before its price rises again. You pause for a minute to take into account two facts, and then to ask yourself a question.

The first fact is: The P-E ratio for this stock is usually 20. In other words, this is its "normal" P-E ratio—in much the same way that a person's temperature is normally 98.6 degrees.

The second fact is: The P-E ratio for this stock today is 40.

The question is: If the normal P-E ratio for this stock is 20 and the current P-E ratio for this stock is 40, then what is the likelihood that something has happened to change the normal P-E ratio for this stock? Stated differently, if what we witness is different from what we normally witness, how likely is it that what we are witnessing is the emergence of a new normal?

Thinking in terms of a ratio—particularly the P-E ratio—grounds us. For the price of a stock to rise because the earnings of the company that issued the stock have been rising is one thing. For the price of a stock to rise even when the earnings of the company that issued the stock are unchanged is a very different thing.

A ratio like a P-E ratio might be called a "will-it-last" ratio. When the price of stock X rises month after month, a person naturally asks, "Will it last?" If a will-it-last ratio—such as the P-E ratio—is consistently rising above its natural level and there seems to be no solid economic reason why this is happening, then the answer is likely to be no.

ANOTHER WILL-IT-LAST RATIO

Just as stock prices can rise month and after month (with no end in sight), so can house prices. Suppose the median price of a house in your area has risen by 25 percent a year for five years straight. Someone says, "You had better buy a house today because next year house prices will be higher."

Will house prices continue to rise? Again, a will-it-last ratio can help answer this question. This will-it-last ratio is the ratio of the percentage change in median house price to the percentage change in income:

$$\frac{\text{Percentage change in median house price}}{\text{Percentage change in income}}$$

Now, suppose this ratio is usually about 1. In other words, the median house price usually rises by the same percentage as the change in income. If income rises by 10 percent, then the median house price rises by 10 percent, and so on. Then, for a period of a few months, the ratio rises to 2, then to 3, then to 4, then to 5. In other words, when the ratio is 5, the percentage change in the median house price is five times the percentage change in income.

Will the ratio stay at 5? Will it rise to 6, and then to 7, and so on? Again, we have to ask ourselves how likely it is that we are witnessing the emergence of a new normal.

BUDDHA'S RATIO

Economists are not the only people who compute ratios. Physicists, chemists, sociologists, and accountants compute ratios too.

Let's consider a ratio that Buddha might have computed. Buddha was interested in personal fulfillment and happiness. Buddha told us that life is suffering and that the reason we suffer is because we often crave things. In terms of a ratio, Buddha was saying this:

$$\text{Degree of suffering} = \frac{\text{What you want}}{\text{What you have}}$$

If what you want (the numerator) is less than what you have (the denominator), then your degree of suffering is less than 1 (good). If what you want is equal to what you have, then your degree of suffering is 1 (good, but not as good as having it less than 1). If what you want is greater than what you have, your degree of suffering is greater than 1 (bad).

How do you suffer less? According to Buddha's ratio, the answer is to want less or have more. Notice we said "have more," not "want more." So, if I were to give you more than you currently have, you would suffer less. Or, if you were to want less than what you have, you would suffer less. Good luck.

FINDING YOUR OWN RATIOS

Economists are fond of saying that even people who think they do not build theories nevertheless build theories. Similarly, even though many people say they do not think in terms of ratios, they often do. When Bob says that he needs to exercise 1 hour for every 3 hours he sits at his desk or else he doesn't feel good, he is really saying that his exercising-to-sitting ratio needs to be at least $\frac{1}{3}$. ("My ratio was $\frac{1}{6}$ today; no wonder I feel out of sorts.")

A useful and enjoyable pastime is to try to identify the ratios you often use. What is your exercising-to-sitting ratio? your watching television-to-studying ratio? your savings-to-income ratio?

What the Economist Thinks

- *One number, by itself, often doesn't provide as much information as one number compared with another.*

- *Economists often think in terms of and compute ratios.* For example, when an economist says that markets are only in equilibrium when, at a given price, quantity demanded equals quantity supplied, she is simply saying that the quantity demanded-quantity supplied ratio is 1.

Questions to Answer

1. Identify five ratios that are important to you in your everyday life.

2. Jack says that sometimes he is depressed and other times he is not. Is some ratio changing for Jack such that when it changes one way, Jack is depressed, but when it changes a different way, he isn't? If so, what might that ratio be?

3. Nancy's grandfather recently said to her, "Back when I was 20 years old, I earned $400 a month, and that was a lot of money then." Is Nancy's grandfather thinking in terms of a ratio? What ratio?

4. Economists often say that individuals think and act in terms of costs and benefits. If benefits are in the numerator and costs are in the denominator, what specifically do economists say about behavior and this ratio? For example, what happens when the ratio is greater than 1? What happens when the ratio is less than 1?

5. Some people have a high listening-to-speaking ratio, while other people have a low listening-to-speaking ratio. Which are you? Do your friends fall exclusively into one category or the other? Some people have a high consuming-to-income ratio, while other people have a low consuming-to-income ratio? Which are you? Do you think your ratio here will change over time? Explain your answer.

chapter 22

More Than Common Sense Is Needed

Common sense is a little like pornography. It is hard to define, but everyone knows what it is when he sees it. (Is this pornography? Not really. What about this? Oh, yes, that's pornography.)

No doubt common sense has saved people from making ridiculous errors of judgment and from accepting arguments that were untrue. Common sense is a useful tool, and the man or woman with common sense certainly has an advantage over the man or woman without it.

But common sense is sometimes not enough. To understand economics and to differentiate between the economically true and the economically false, you need more than common sense.

How Would You Answer This Question?

Suppose there are two people, Jim and Bob, each of whom can produce two goods, A and B. Jim can produce the following combinations of the two goods.

Combination	Good A	Good B
1	90	0
2	60	10
3	30	20
4	0	30

Bob can produce the following combinations of the two goods.

Combination	Good A	Good B
1'	15	0
2'	10	5
3'	5	10
4'	0	15

In the time it takes Bob to produce 15 units of good A, Jim can produce 90 units. In the time it takes Bob to produce 15 units of good B, Jim can produce 30 units. Obviously, Jim is better than Bob at producing both goods. We can say that Jim is Bob's superior in producing both goods or that Bob is Jim's inferior in producing both goods.

Now, suppose all you can use is common sense to answer this question: Because Jim can produce more of both goods A and B than Bob can, is there any benefit to Jim of trading with Bob? What does your common sense tell you? Your common sense would lead you to answer no to this question. But your common sense would lead you to the wrong answer.

Many years ago, English economist David Ricardo showed how a person who could do two activities better than another person could still benefit by trading with that person. Ricardo's proof, a simple one, is described in the following paragraphs.

Let's look again at the situation for Jim. Viewing the combinations of the two goods that he can produce, we realize that the opportunity cost (to him) of producing 1 unit of A is $\frac{1}{3}$ unit of B. This means Jim's opportunity cost of producing 1 unit of B is 3 units of A.

Now, let's compute the opportunity cost of producing each good for Bob. We see that Bob's opportunity cost of producing 1 unit of A is 1 unit of B.

Who is the low cost producer of A? Jim can produce 1 unit of A at a cost of $\frac{1}{3}$ unit of B, and Bob can produce 1 unit of A at a cost of 1 unit of B. So, Jim is the low cost producer of A. He has, according to the economist, the comparative advantage in producing good A.

Who is the low cost producer of B? Jim can produce 1 unit of B at a cost of 3 units of A, and Bob can produce 1 unit of B at a cost of 1 unit of A. So, Bob is the low cost producer of B. His comparative advantage is in producing good B.

We conclude: Although Jim is better than Bob at producing both A and B, Jim's superiority over Bob is greater when producing A than when producing B. (When compared to his gardener, an attorney can be better both at providing legal advice and at mowing the lawn, but still the attorney might be much better than his gardener at providing legal advice and only slightly better than his gardener at mowing the lawn.)

Suppose both Jim and Bob specialize in producing the good for which each has the comparative advantage; that is, Jim produces only A, and Bob produces only B. Jim, then, produces 90 units of A, and Bob produces 15 units of B.

Furthermore, suppose Jim and Bob trade some of what each produces for some of what the other produces. What might be acceptable terms of trade for the two men? One set of acceptable terms of trade would be 20 units of *A* for 10 units of *B*.

Let's summarize the situation for Jim and Bob:

1. Jim is better than Bob at producing both *A* and *B*.

2. Jim has the comparative advantage in producing *A*; Bob has the comparative advantage in producing *B*.

3. Each man specializes in producing the good in which he has the comparative advantage: Jim produces only *A*; Bob produces only *B*.

4. Jim produces 90 units of *A* and trades 20 of these units to Bob, in return receiving 10 units of *B* from Bob. Jim ends up with 70 units of *A* and 10 units of *B* to consume.

5. Bob produces 15 units of *B* and trades 10 of these units to Jim, in return receiving 20 units of *A* from Jim. Bob ends up with 20 units of *A* and 5 units of *B* to consume.

The question we ask now—the question Ricardo focused on—is: Are both men better off specializing and trading than not specializing and not trading, even if one man can produce more of both goods than the other can?

To find the answer, we have to determine how much each man would consume if he did not specialize and trade. Obviously, if Jim and Bob did not trade, each man would produce and consume one of the four combinations of goods set out earlier. That is, Jim would produce and consume combination 1 (90 units of *A* and 0 units of *B*), 2, 3, or 4. Bob would produce and consume combination 1' (15 units of *A* and 0 units of *B*), 2', 3', or 4'. Each man likely would want to consume some of both goods *A* and *B* ("man does not live by bread alone"). So, Jim would produce either combination 2 or combination 3, and Bob would produce either combination 2' or combination 3'.

Let's assume that Jim would produce combination 2 and that Bob would produce combination 2'. Thus, if neither man specializes and trades, Jim would produce and consume 60 units of *A* and 10 units of *B* and Bob would produce and consume 10 units of *A* and 5 units of *B*.

So, are both men better off specializing and trading than not specializing and not trading? Bob, the inferior producer of both goods, is better off because he can consume more of good *A* (20 units instead of 10 units) and no less of good *B* (5 units in either case). But what about Jim, who is Bob's superior in producing both *A* and *B*? Is it worthwhile for Jim to trade with Bob? Certainly it is. The added benefits are being able to consume 10 more units of *A* (70 units instead of 60 units) and no less of good *B* (10 units in either case). Thus, dealing with his inferior makes Jim better off.

Would common sense have led us to this conclusion? Probably not—the results of Ricardo's arguments are counterintuitive. But, then, so is much of economics.

WHY DIDN'T RICARDO SIMPLY RELY ON HIS COMMON SENSE? OR, HOW CAN WE BECOME RICARDIANS?

Ricardo obviously used more than his common sense to show how a person who could do two activities better than another person could still benefit by trading with that person. Why didn't he simply rely on his common sense? What was it that pushed him beyond his common sense?

We don't know for sure, but it could have been simple observation. Recall the lawyer who is better than a gardener at providing attorney services and at mowing lawns—yet he hires the gardener to mow his lawn. Perhaps Ricardo, who is reported to have been a very bright fellow, saw himself doing the same thing as the lawyer. Maybe Ricardo realized he was better than almost everyone at doing X, Y, and Z, but found himself only doing X and hiring others to do Y and Z. Perhaps Ricardo scratched his head one day and tried to figure out why, if he was better than others at doing X, Y, and Z, he chose to do only X and not Y and Z too.

If things did happen this way for Ricardo, he must have thought that he stumbled onto a puzzle of sorts. Being the type of person who liked to solve puzzles, Ricardo might have sat down with pen and paper and tried to solve the puzzle. His solution—which is called the **law of comparative advantage**—is studied by economics students today.

Maybe the way to become a Ricardian is to look for life's puzzles. Why does a person who is better at both X and Y do only X and hire someone to do Y? Why do interest rates sometimes rise and sometimes fall? Why are some nations rich and other nations poor? Why do movie theaters charge a higher admission fee at night than during the afternoon?

ADAM SMITH HAD A PUZZLE TOO

Adam Smith, the father of modern economics, liked to look at the world around him and ask questions. He liked to try to solve life's puzzles. One puzzle that Smith wanted to solve was: Why is water, which people need to survive, much cheaper than diamonds, which people do not need to survive?

We can restate Smith's puzzle, which is called the **diamond-water paradox**, as: Why does something that has high value in use (such as water) have a low exchange value (or price), while something that has low value in use (such as a diamond) have a high exchange value (or price)? Doesn't common sense tell you it should be the opposite? After all, isn't it reasonable (commonsensical?) to assume that something you can't live without should be priced higher than something you can live without?

But, here again, following our common sense takes us down the wrong road. The solution to the diamond-water paradox is that even though water is more useful (to life) than diamonds, diamonds are priced higher because price is a reflection of marginal utility, not total utility.

The law of diminishing marginal utility states that as one consumes additional units of a good, each successive unit provides less utility than the unit that preceded it. The tenth unit of water provides less utility than the ninth, the ninth provides less utility than the eighth, and so on. Similarly, the tenth diamond provides less utility than the ninth, the ninth provides less utility than the eighth, and so on.

When we buy water, we do not buy all the water in the world; we buy an additional unit of water. Now is this "additional unit" the 2d unit, 100th unit, or 1,000th unit? For a good like water that is in plentiful supply, the additional unit might be the 1,000th unit (which has lower marginal utility than the 999th unit, which, of course, has lower marginal utility than the 998th unit, and so on). In other words, it is very likely that our additional unit of water has low marginal utility because we have bought so much water previously. We pay a relatively low price for an additional unit of a good that brings low marginal utility. Thus, we pay a relatively low price for water.

Diamonds are not as plentiful as water. So, when we buy an additional diamond, we are not likely buying our 1,000th diamond, but perhaps only our 2d. Because we have purchased so few diamonds, an additional diamond is likely to bring high marginal utility. We pay a relatively high price for an additional unit of a good that brings high marginal utility. Thus, we pay a relatively high price for diamonds.

The solution to the diamond-water paradox is counterintuitive—it goes against our intuition. It went against Smith's intuition, which told him that water should be more expensive than diamonds because water is more useful (to life) than diamonds are. But, then, his eyes told him something different. He saw diamonds selling for more than water. Obviously, when our intuition and our observations do not agree, we have a puzzle of sorts that needs to be solved. Smith did not solve the diamond-water paradox. That puzzle was left for the marginal utility economists (such as Bentham, Jevons, and others) to solve.

COMMON SENSE AND A RATIO

Let's consider two countries, the United States and Mexico. Wages in the United States are relatively high compared to wages in Mexico. Will U.S. companies want to hire American labor or Mexican labor?

Many people answer "Mexican labor." They explain their answer by first pointing out that U.S. companies want their costs to be as low as possible because they want their profits to be as high as possible. They then say that U.S. companies can keep their costs down by hiring Mexican labor instead of American labor.

This answer makes perfect common sense. After all, no one doubts that U.S. companies want to earn profits, and no one doubts that Mexican labor is cheaper than American labor. So, it "makes sense" to tie the two together and conclude that U.S. companies will want to hire Mexican labor rather than American labor.

The only problem with this answer is that it's wrong. U.S. companies don't necessarily want to hire Mexican labor. Even when they can hire Mexican labor, U.S. companies sometimes choose not to do so.

Obviously, common sense, or intuition, is at odds with reality. Why has common sense once again led us astray?

Perhaps we should be thinking like economists—in terms of ratios—instead of relying on common sense. If reality cannot be explained by comparing two single dollar amounts—wages in the U.S. and wages in Mexico—maybe single dollar amounts are the wrong variables. Maybe we ought to consider ratios instead.

The relevant ratio in this case is the wage-to-productivity ratio. The only thing that could offset higher U.S. wages for U.S. companies is higher U.S. productivity. For example, suppose the average American earns $20 an hour and can produce 5 units of X in an hour. Suppose the average Mexican, on the other hand, earns $7 an hour and can produce 1 unit of X in an hour. Who is cheaper for the firm to hire? If we look only at the dollar wages, we compare $20 for the American to $7 for the Mexican and conclude that the Mexican worker is cheaper to hire. But if we compare the American wage-to-productivity ratio to the Mexican wage-to-productivity ratio, we see that the American worker is cheaper to hire. (The American produces 5 units of X for $20, or 1 unit of X for $4; the Mexican produces 1 unit of X for $7).

HOW DO I KNOW WHEN I'M WRONG?

The problem with common sense is that it somehow "feels" so right that we often do not look any further for the correct answer. For example, I often ask students in my classes what will happen to a firm's total revenue if the firm raises its price. Almost all students answer that the firm's total revenue will rise. When I ask why, most students say, "It just has to be this way because the firm is selling its product at a higher price."

Obviously, my students are implicitly assuming that the firm will sell the same number of units of its good at the higher price as it did at the lower price. In other words, the students are implicitly assuming that the firm faces a perfectly inelastic demand curve.

After I point out that what happens to total revenue depends on the percentage rise in price related to the percentage fall in quantity demanded, students are quick to get the point. The lesson for the students, and for everyone else, is that we can't always trust our common sense. Common sense is sometimes not enough.

To understand economics, we need to "test" our common sense. We have to ask ourselves, just as economists do: If I'm wrong, how will I know? To illustrate, suppose Jack thinks it is obvious that when a firm raises its price, its total revenue rises too. This is what Jack's common sense tells him. How would economists proceed to "test" Jack's common sense? Primarily in two ways:

1. *Deduce what is logically consistent from what is assumed to be true.* Jack believes that every time a firm raises its price, the firm's total revenue rises too. Well if Jack is right, what logically follows? The answer is that we would expect to see firms raise price on Monday, and again on Tuesday, and once again on Wednesday, and so on. Why not? After all, if every time a firm raises its price its total revenue rises too, then firms would never stop raising prices. So, what logical conclusion do we deduce from what Jack believes to be true? We deduce that the price of every good and service must be somewhere in the millions of dollars. All we have to do now is simply ask: Do we see computers, books, cars, shoes, and all other goods selling for millions of dollars? The answer is no, which gives us reason to question Jack's belief that when a firm raises its price, its total revenue necessarily rises.

2. *Collect the Data.* Another way to proceed is to identify firms that have raised price in the last year or so and see what happened to their total revenue as a result. Is it the case that for every firm that raised price, total revenue went up?[1] If not, then Jack is wrong that every time a firm raises price its total revenue rises. (By the way, it does not follow that Jack is right if total revenue had risen for each firm that raised price. It could simply have been that the firms that raised price faced an inelastic demand curve. If a firm that faced an elastic demand curve had raised price, its total revenue would have fallen.)

---

1 We are assuming here that when the price and total revenue data are collected every attempt is being made to hold other things constant.

- *Common sense is not always guaranteed to provide the correct answers to questions.* In short, common sense is not enough.

- *We must always test our common sense.* In other words, we must try to figure out if we are wrong about what we think is true. We can do this in either of two ways. In the first way, we simply deduce what is logically consistent from what we have assumed to be true; then we test what we have deduced against the facts. (Step 1: If X is true, then Y must be true too. Step 2: Is Y true?) In the second way, we collect (real-world) data to see whether or not the data support what we say is true.

Questions to Answer

1. Imagine you are living during the years 1200–1250. A man comes up to you and says that the earth is round. Would your common sense tell you that what the man says is correct or incorrect? Explain your answer.

2. Give an example of your common sense having led you astray. Could you have tested your common sense in either of the two ways discussed in this chapter? If so, how would you have tested your common sense?

3. Where do you see the law of comparative advantage in everyday life?

4. If common sense doesn't always give us the right answers, then why do you think so many of us like common sense as much as we do?

5. Zee says that when she gets more money, she is better off, so it's just common sense to believe that if everyone gets more money, everyone will be better off. Do you agree with Zee? Do you think it is true that more money for everyone means everyone will be better off? If so, how would you know if you were wrong?

chapter 23

Did I Ask for This?
Would I Have Asked for This?

Economists know that people can want different things at different times. For example, you might want to eat ice cream on Tuesday and to have a good figure on Wednesday. But, of course, you have a problem: too much ice cream on Tuesday makes a good figure on Wednesday less likely. Or, you might want to watch television and socialize with friends on Thursday and to get a high grade on your math test on Friday. Again, you have a problem: too much television watching and socializing on Thursday might make a high grade on Friday less likely.

In a sense, everyone has a "short-run self" and a "long-run self." When these two selves want things that conflict with each other, and they often do, a person must choose one self over the other self. Do you choose your short-run self or your long-run self? the ice cream eating self or the self that wants a good figure? the television watching and socializing self or the self that wants a high grade?

Even if you choose your long-run self over your short-run self, you are not guaranteed to get what your long-run self wants. Sometimes your short-run self is pretty strong. Your short-run self might say, "I know you want me to go away, but you have overlooked the fact that I'm not a weakling. When you least expect it—when you're tired or not thinking about me or when your willpower is in short supply—I'll show up. And I'm likely to get my way."

If you realize that your short-run self is right and that you are not strong enough to fight it alone, you might ask for a constraint to be placed on you. Of course, you only want the constraint placed on your short-run self—the part of you acting in a way that is contrary to the wishes of your long-run self.

To illustrate, let's consider Kevin, who smokes too many cigarettes. Kevin realizes that he is really two people—a short-run Kevin and a long-run Kevin. The short-run Kevin wants to smoke a cigarette whenever he gets the urge, which he usually gets 30 times a day. The long-run Kevin wants cleaner, healthier lungs and a longer life. The long-run Kevin hates the short-run Kevin as much as the short-run Kevin hates the long-run Kevin.

Suppose Kevin chooses his long-run self and is determined to make his short-run self take a back seat. To help his long-run self, Kevin tells his wife, Kathy, to never buy any cigarettes for him, to take his cigarettes away from him if she finds him with any cigarettes, and to never give him a cigarette no matter how much he pleads for one. Kathy agrees to do what Kevin asks.

A week passes and Kevin hasn't smoked a cigarette. But then he can't take it any longer: he has to have a cigarette to smoke. He asks Kathy for a cigarette. She says no. He asks again. She tells him that he told her never to give him a cigarette. He says that he knows what he told her but has changed his mind because quitting smoking is harder than he thought it would be. Kevin tells Kathy that life is short and should be enjoyed, so she should give him a cigarette. Kathy refuses. Kevin goes away angry with Kathy. He thinks she is too rigid and stubborn.

But, of course, Kevin doesn't have a good reason for being angry with Kathy; she is simply doing what Kevin asked her to do. He wanted her to be rigid and stubborn—rigid and stubborn in not giving him any cigarettes.

WE SOMETIMES CONSTRAIN OURSELVES FOR A GOOD REASON

We are accustomed to thinking that fewer constraints are better than more constraints. We are accustomed to believing that no one would ever ask for someone to constrain him. Asking to be constrained is like asking to eat mud, to sleep on a bed of nails, or to be placed in prison. People just don't ask for such things.

Granted, people don't ask for bads (things that give them disutility or dissatisfaction) unless, of course, the bads make it easier to acquire certain goods. No one would ask for the flu (a bad) if asking for the flu simply resulted in getting the flu. But someone might ask for the flu (a bad) if getting the flu also meant getting $500 (a good).

People tend to believe that any bad visited on them is done so without their consent. But economists know this isn't always true. Economists know the one question we should ask ourselves when a bad appears in our lives is: *Did I ask for this?*

For example, Kevin is angry with Kathy for not giving him a cigarette. He is angry with her for not understanding what he is going through and how much he needs to smoke. For Kevin, Kathy's behavior toward him is a bad. To more clearly understand why this bad appeared in his life, Kevin needs to ask himself: *Did I ask for this?* Kevin should realize that the answer is yes, which should then provide Kevin with a more accurate perspective regarding Kathy's behavior toward him.

Do Students Want Challenging Exams?

Students often complain about challenging exams. If asked whether they prefer a challenging exam or an easy exam, students almost always say that they prefer an easy exam. Thus, students often view a challenging exam as a bad. Consequently, students view the person who writes and delivers the challenging exam to them—that is, the professor—as a "bad person." (Recall that Kevin viewed Kathy as a "bad person" too. But we know she wasn't because we were there when Kevin asked her to deny him a cigarette should he ask for one.)

College students don't just complain about challenging exams when asked. They are also unlikely to come to the professor at the beginning of the semester and say, "Professor, part of us wants you to give easy exams, and part of us wants you to give challenging exams. The part that wants easy exams cares only about grades and doing as little work as possible. The part that wants challenging exams cares about learning as much as possible. The part that wants easy exams will often overcome the part that wants to learn as much as possible (especially in the middle of the semester or near the end of the semester), so we want to enlist your help in winning this battle the way it should be won. No matter how often we come to you during the semester and complain about challenging exams, and no matter how many times we complain about you for giving us challenging exams, we want you to ignore us and give us challenging exams."

However, even though college students do not utter these words to their professors, they might want to. I have often heard students complain about a course because the exams were too easy and they thought they weren't learning enough. So, some evidence exists that students might not want easy exams and professors.

What question would economists say students should ask themselves when given a challenging exam? When Kathy denies Kevin a cigarette, economists believe Kevin should ask himself: *Did I ask for this?* Similarly, when a professor gives her students a challenging exam and the students begin to grumble, they should ask: *Would I have asked for this?* If their answer is yes, then they should understand that things are really the way they want them to be.

ARE SPEEDING TICKETS A BAD?

No one who gets a speeding ticket is happy about it. Speeding tickets are always seen as bads—as something that gives the driver disutility or dissatisfaction. And almost always, the police officer who writes the speeding ticket is castigated for "not spending his time searching out the real criminals in society."

So, a driver who speeds and receives a traffic ticket for speeding believes a bad has appeared in her life. What is the relevant question for the speeder to ask? According to economists, the question is: Would I have asked for a speeding ticket?

The answer, under certain conditions, is yes. To understand why, suppose we leave the world in which we live and imagine that we live in a different world. In this imaginary world, roads and freeways still exist and drivers in cars still go from one place to another. However, there are no speed limit laws and no police officers to apprehend speeders and write speeding tickets.

Will many of the drivers in this imaginary world speed? No doubt they will because the cost of speeding is relatively low. Of course, a world in which drivers often drive too fast is a relatively unsafe world. If 90 out of 100 drivers are speeding, we can expect frequent crashes and deaths.

At some point, the drivers in our imaginary world are likely to come together to try to make their world safer. They think of several possible solutions, but none seem workable until someone proposes that speed limits be posted. Immediately, someone else proposes that everyone promise to obey the posted speed limits. All the drivers think that the idea of speed limits is a good idea, and everyone promises to obey the speed limits. This solution works for about a day. Then, someone realizes that she is better off if she speeds and no one else speeds, so she speeds. But, of course, what one person can think, others can too. Soon everyone is speeding again. Everyone is speeding again even though there are posted speed limits and everyone promised not to speed.

In time, everyone realizes that posted speed limits and promises are not enough. People will speed as long as there is no one to enforce the speed limit. Everyone will speed as long as no one is punished for speeding.

The way to move from our imaginary world where everyone speeds and the roads are unsafe to a world where few people speed and the roads are safe is to enact an enforcement-penalty system. In and of itself, an enforcement-penalty system is a bad. It is like asking for a daily whipping. But a daily whipping might not be so bad if it prevents an even worse bad (death in the streets). In other words, all drivers might be better off living in a world where police officers stop speeders and give them tickets than living in a world where there are no speed limits, no police officers, and no speeding tickets.

Suppose Jack has just been stopped for speeding at the corner of Third and Main. Jack grabs the ticket out the officer's hand and goes on his way, trembling with anger. Underneath his breath, he is cursing the police officer. Would Jack have asked for the ticket?

BOSSES AND WORKERS

Bob works 40 hours a week for a company that produces furniture. Bob says that his boss, Carl, is always watching him and his fellow workers, making sure that they get to work on time, don't take lunch breaks that are too long, and so on. "It kind of gets on your nerves after a while," he says.

Did Bob ask for this? No. Would he have under certain circumstances? Yes, he might have. To understand under what circumstances he might have, let's consider an economist's story—one about people making furniture.[1]

Suppose five people, *A–E*, each works alone making furniture. Each person makes 10 pieces of furniture a day. So, the five individuals (each working alone) produce a total of 50 pieces of furniture a day.

Could the five individuals produce more furniture a day if they worked together? If they can, they have an incentive to work together and form a small business firm. Whenever individuals working together can produce more than the sum of what they can produce working alone, they have an incentive to work together. In short, they have an incentive to form a firm.

Let's suppose that the five individuals can produce 100 pieces of furniture a day if they work together. So, our five individuals form a firm, produce 100 pieces of furniture a day, and split the proceeds equally. In other words, each person gets the sales revenue from 20 pieces of furniture.

Obviously, it looks like the five individuals have made a good choice. But, let's consider what might happen on any given day in the firm. Suppose one day, *A* decides to come to work late, take a long lunch break, and leave work early—simply put, *A* decides to shirk. As a result of *A*'s shirking, the firm does not produce 100 pieces of furniture on this day; instead, it produces only 90 pieces of furniture. Dividing the sales revenue from 90 pieces of furniture among five individuals results in each individual receiving the revenue from 18 pieces of furniture.

---

1 The scenario presented here is implicit in the theory of the firm as presented by Armen Alchian and Harold Demsetz. See "Production, Information Costs, and Economic Organization," *American Economic Review* 62 (December 1972): 777-95.

Notice what has happened. *A* did all the shirking and received all the benefits of his shirking, but the cost of his shirking (10 fewer pieces of furniture) was spread over all five individuals in the firm. That is, *A* paid one-fifth of the cost of his shirking, and his coworkers paid the other four-fifths.

Would *A* have been as likely to shirk if he were working for himself? If he were working for himself, *A* would still receive all the benefits of his shirking but he would pay all the costs too. It is likely that *A* will shirk less when he can't spread the costs of his shirking over others than when he can. Simply put, there is likely to be more shirking in a group setting than in a one-person setting.

Of course, what holds for *A* holds for *B*, *C*, *D*, and *E* too. Each of the individuals is likely to find shirking cheaper in a group, and so each is likely to shirk more in a group setting than in a one-person setting.

The five individuals in our firm now have a problem. They came together and formed a firm because they could produce more as a firm than the sum of what they could produce working alone. But, after they formed the firm, they began shirking, thereby eliminating some of the additional output that was the reason for their forming the firm. For example, if the additional output from forming the firm is 50 pieces of furniture, then shirking is reducing this to 40 pieces, then perhaps 30 pieces, then perhaps 20 pieces, and so on.

Obviously, something has to be done about the shirking. The individuals in the firm decide that one among them must be the monitor of the others. His job will be to make sure the others do not shirk. They choose *B* as the monitor. Now without *B* producing furniture, furniture output will decline. But it may be better for everyone if furniture output declines a little rather than a lot.

Suppose with *B* as monitor, output declines from 100 pieces of furniture each day to 85 pieces. Dividing the sales revenue from 85 pieces of furniture over five individuals is still be better than what each individual received each day working alone (revenue from 17 pieces of furniture instead of from 10 pieces).

As monitor, *B* can fire shirkers and replace them with (one hopes) nonshirkers. But, then, how can the other four individuals be sure that the monitor won't shirk? Well, they can't be sure unless *B* has an incentive not to shirk. So, the other four individuals give *B* this incentive by making him the residual claimant: the person who earns the firm's profit or incurs its losses. In other words, individuals *A*, *C*, *D*, and *E* contract for some "wage" greater than they would have earned working for themselves and essentially say to *B* that he can have everything over the contracted costs. Now, *B* has an incentive to not shirk. If he shirks, others will get away with their shirking; and if too many others get away with their shirking, output will fall and *B* will be less likely to earn a profit.

Now let's return to Bob, working at the furniture company and complaining about his boss watching him too closely. Might he want his boss (his monitor) to make sure that he and the other workers do not shirk? Might he have asked for the constraint that his boss represents?

What the Economist Thinks

- *Sometimes what our short-run self wants conflicts with what our long-run self wants.* We might want *X* this year and *Y* next year, but getting *X* this year precludes our getting *Y* next year.

- *A large part of economics deals with the choices that individuals make.* (Do I buy 10 apples and 5 oranges or 5 apples and 10 oranges? Do I go to college or begin working right after high school?) Sometimes individuals will elect to constrain themselves so that a particular choice can be realized.

Questions and Answers

1. Identify three constraints in your life that you may have (at least) implicitly agreed to.

2. "People who impose constraints on themselves are usually more long-run oriented than people who do not." Do you agree or disagree with this statement? Explain your answer.

3. Do you think people have free will as far as choosing between their short-run selves and their long-run selves? Explain your answer

4. Diets often do not work because they do not include an enforcement-penalty system. Consider the following possible system: A man who wants to lose 40 pounds gives $10,000 to person *X*. Person *X* agrees to return the money only if the man loses 40 pounds within a certain period of time. Assuming that person *X* can be trusted to give back the money if the man loses the weight and to keep the money if the man does not lose the weight, do you think this enforcement-penalty system would work? If so, then why don't we see more "diet plans" with such an enforcement-penalty mechanism? Are there any current diet plans that come close to having a enforcement-penalty system similar to the one described here?

5. When Jennifer pays her income taxes each year, she usually complains about the amount she pays. Specifically, she thinks that she pays too much of her income in taxes. Do you think Jennifer is grumbling about the amount of taxes she pays or about the fact that she has to pay any taxes at all? Would individuals ask for taxes? Explain your answers.

chapter 24

Right for Me, Right for You, But Wrong for Us

Suppose ten people have two options, *A* and *B*. Every one of the ten people ranks *A* before *B*, and so everyone chooses *A* over *B*. Most people would believe that because everyone chooses *A*, everyone gets *A*.

But sometimes when everyone chooses *A*, everyone gets *B*. In other words, everyone chooses his top choice over his second choice, but somehow because everyone does this, everyone's second choice emerges. We can state the phenomenon this way: You choose what is right for you, I choose what is right for me, and we get what is wrong for both of us.

To illustrate, suppose 500 people are crowded into a nightclub when a fire starts. Each person in the nightclub has two options: run to the nearest exit or walk to the nearest exit. Each person ranks running as superior to walking—each person thinks he will get out of the nightclub faster if he runs than he will if he walks. But if everyone runs, there is a greater chance that fewer individuals will get out of the nightclub safely. In other words, if everyone chooses the better course of action (running instead of walking) everyone (or nearly everyone) ends up with an inferior outcome (getting hurt).

Thinking in terms of "individual actions" and "group outcomes" is the best way to understand this phenomenon. Sometimes in life the best individual action leads to the best group outcome, and sometimes the best individual action leads to the second-best group outcome (which may or may not be the worst group outcome). The next two sections provide examples of the best individual action leading to the second-best group outcome.

THE COLD WAR

During the Cold War, both the United States and the Soviet Union complained about the arms race. Each country said that it had to proceed with a military buildup because the other country was proceeding with a military buildup.

Every now and then, leaders of the two countries would meet and talk about arms control. The United States would agree to reduce its armaments (or reduce the rate of increasing its armaments) if the Soviet Union did the same. The Soviet Union often agreed.

After the two countries entered into an arms agreement, each country had two options: hold to the arms agreement or break the arms agreement. The better course of action was to break the arms agreement because if one country broke the agreement and the other did not, the one that broke the agreement would achieve military superiority. (Each country seemed to rank military superiority over equality.)

Of course, as a result of each country choosing its better option (break the agreement), the outcome was a continuation of the military buildup—just what the two countries said they wanted to discontinue.

Before you criticize the two countries' actions, consider how hard it would have been to act differently. Was the United States really likely to have chosen its second-best choice, knowing that if the Soviet Union chose its first-best choice, the United States might end up worse off than before it had entered into the arms agreement? And doesn't the same hold for the Soviet Union?

DISNEYLAND

Disneyland opens at 10 o'clock in the morning. Assuming that a person wants to spend the whole day at Disneyland, the best time to get to the park is 30 seconds before it opens. Getting to the park 30 seconds before it opens is better than getting to the park anywhere between, say, 1 minute and 30 minutes after it opens.

Of course, if everyone chooses the best course of action (30 seconds early instead of somewhere between 1 minute and 30 minutes late), then a huge crowd of people will be waiting outside the park 30 seconds before it opens. In fact, one might have to wait longer than 30 minutes to get into the park.

Everyone waiting to get into the park is thinking: "I took the best course of action—30 seconds early instead of somewhere between 1 minute and 30 minutes late. But everyone else took the same course of action for the same reason I did. So, many of us will now get into the park later than we would have had we taken something other than the best course of action."

SELF-INTEREST AND GROUP OUTCOME

An earlier chapter discusses how money emerged from a barter economy. Recall that in a barter economy, where trade was time-consuming and difficult, each individual decided to do what was in his or her best interest: accept the good, among all goods, that was most likely to be accepted in trade. Through this process, money emerged;

and with money's emergence, people gained a higher standard of living. In short, the story of money's emergence is a story of self-interested individual actions producing a positive group outcome.

However, now you know that sometimes self-interested individual actions produce a negative group outcome. Might it be possible for people to somehow avoid self-interested individual actions when the actions will lead to a negative group outcome?

Suppose we think in science-fiction terms. Imagine that everyone is born with an internal mechanism that senses whether self-interest will lead to a positive outcome or to a negative outcome. When a person is in a setting where self-interest will lead to a negative outcome, the internal mechanism turns off self-interest. When a person is in a setting where self-interest will lead to a positive outcome, the internal mechanism turns on self-interest.

What would the internal mechanism have done in the case of the fire in the crowded nightclub? It would have turned off self-interest. Instead of running to the nearest exit, everyone would have walked.

But, alas, people do not have an internal mechanism that turns self-interest on and off. The switch is almost always turned on. Sometimes this leads to positive outcomes, and sometimes it leads to negative outcomes.

An economist realizes that self-interest multiplied across thousands of individuals sometimes gives people what everyone wants and sometimes gives people just the opposite of what everyone wants. An economist also realizes that no amount of talk is likely to be effective at getting people to switch off their self-interest. (It's sort of like trying to convince a person to switch off his appetite or his need for sleep. Talk all you want, it isn't going to happen. Thousands of years of evolutionary hard-wiring are difficult to overcome by talking and wishing.)

ANALYSIS OF A NEGATIVE OUTCOME—THE FREE RIDER

Suppose there are two groups, one small and one large. The small group consists of 10,000 individuals, and the large group consists of 100 million people. The small group goes to the U.S. Congress and urges passage of a bill that would effectively take $300 million from the members of the large group and give the money to the members of the small group.

At first glance, you might think that the members of Congress would turn a deaf ear to the proposal. However, they might not because the proponents of the bill—the members of the small group—are likely to be much more visible to the members of Congress than the members of the large group are.

Why will the members of the small group be more visible? If the bill passes, the average member of the small group will receive $30,000

($300 million divided by the 10,000 persons in the small group), while the average member of the large group will lose $3. An individual is likely to scream louder to get $30,000 than to keep $3.

But the real question is: Will the average member of the large group scream at all? There is good reason to believe that he won't.

To explain why, suppose Mr. Jones, one member of the large group, sends a letter to all 100 million members of the large group. He writes:

Dear Members of the Large Group:

No doubt you have heard about the actions of the members of the small group. They are trying to get our elected representatives to take $300 million away from us and put it into their pockets. This is a mad grab for money and we must fight it. If we don't, we are just rolling over and letting the members of the small group steal our money.

I would like to hire a few lobbyists to go to Washington, D.C., and argue our case. But lobbyists cost money. I am asking each of you to send me only 25 cents. If everyone sends 25 cents, then we will have $25 million to fight the small group.

Please send your checks for 25 cents to me at the following address ...

Signed,
Mr. Jones

Now suppose you know that Mr. Jones is a dedicated and honest person. You know he will use the money that people send him to do just what he has said he wants to do. He won't pocket one penny of the money sent to him.

So, will you send him 25 cents? Probably not. You will likely say to yourself: "If I don't send my 25 cents, the total amount raised by Mr. Jones will be reduced by only one quarter. If Mr. Jones gets a quarter from everyone else but me, he will receive a quarter from 99,999,999 people. Do you mean to tell me that if only one person doesn't contribute, Mr. Jones isn't going to proceed with his plan to lobby Washington? Not likely. My contribution is only a drop in the bucket of contributions and doesn't really matter. If it doesn't really matter, why send it?"

So, because your contribution really doesn't matter much, you are likely to choose to become a free rider. A **free rider** is a person who receives the benefits of something without incurring any of the costs.

While the 100 million individuals in our scenario might want to fight the bill that takes $300 million from them, each person recognizes that her contribution to the fight is small and that the fight will likely go on without her. So, each individual is likely to become a free rider. But when everyone becomes a free rider, there is no one to fight what everyone says she wants to fight.

The economist sees the problem of the free rider in terms of individual actions leading to a negative group outcome. The economist

330
A758
132

LINCOLN CHRISTIAN COLLEGE AND SEMINARY
110972

summarizes the scenario described above as follows: Each member of the large group wants to fight the bill that takes money out of his pocket, but when he does what is in his best interest and opts to be a free rider, there is no one to left to fight.

The economist then tries to determine what conditions are necessary for the scenario to turn out differently. He asks: How must things be structured so that the members of a group—all of whom say they want X and are willing to pay to get X—not do what is in their best interest and instead put their money, time, and energy toward getting X? In short, how do you structure things so that free riding doesn't prevent people from getting what they want?

What the Economist Thinks

- *The best individual action can sometimes lead to the best group outcome.*

- *The best individual action can sometimes lead to the second-best group outcome.*

- *When the best individual action leads to the second-best group outcome (instead of the best group outcome), certain questions need to be asked and answered.* These questions include: *Why did the best individual action lead to the second-best group outcome? How can things be structured differently so that the best individual action/ second-best group outcome can be turned into the best individual action/best group outcome?*

Questions to Answer

1. Is an individual more likely to be a free rider if she is a member of a small group or a member of a large group? Explain your answer.

2. A college campus has a sidewalk between two buildings. In addition, a dirt path between the two buildings has emerged over time. The dirt path is the result of students and faculty sometimes walking on the grass between the two buildings instead of walking on the sidewalk. Is the dirt path a second-best outcome that results from a best individual action taken? Explain your answer.

3. Give an example of the best individual action leading to the best group outcome. Next, give an example of the best individual action leading to a second-best group outcome.

4. Speculate on why sometimes the best individual action leads to the best group outcome and at other times it leads to the second-best group outcome.

5. "If one person gets more money, he is better off. But if everyone gets more money, it is not necessarily the case that everyone is better off." Do you agree or disagree with the statement? Explain your answer.

3 4711 00195 0858